LOST RAIL
OF
WILTSHIRE

LOST RAILWAYS
OF
WILTSHIRE

Justin Bailey

COUNTRYSIDE BOOKS
NEWBURY BERKSHIRE

COUNTRYSIDE BOOKS
3 Catherine Road
Newbury, Berkshire

To view our complete range of books,
please visit us at
www.countrysidebooks.co.uk

ISBN 1 85306 993 0
EAN 978 185306 993 2

For Candace

The cover picture shows
the Bristolian Express leaving Box Tunnel,
from an original painting
by Colin Doggett

Produced through The Letterworks Ltd., Reading
Typeset by KT Designs, St Helens
Printed by The Holywell Press, Oxford

CONTENTS

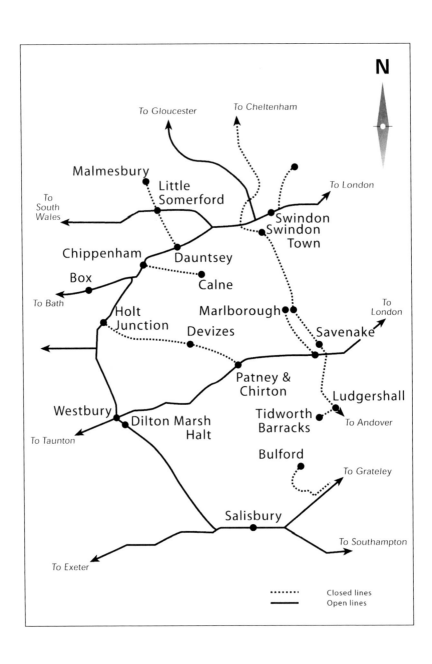

ABBREVIATIONS

The following abbreviations are used in this book:

A&RR	Andover and Redbridge Railway
BR	British Rail
DMU	Diesel Multiple Unit
EMU	Electric Multiple Unit
GWR	Great Western Railway
L&SWR	London & South Western Railway
M&GR	Marlborough and Grafton Railway
MR	Midland Railway
M&SWJR	Midland and South Western Junction Railway
SR&MH Co.	Salisbury Railway and Market House Company Railway
S&CER	Swindon and Cheltenham Extension Railway
S&HR	Swindon and Highworth Railway
SM&AR	Swindon, Marlborough and Andover Railway
SR	Southern Railway
WS&WR	Wiltshire, Somerset and Weymouth Railway

ACKNOWLEDGEMENTS

I would like to thank the following people for helping me with my research: Andy Doran, Chris Turner, Graham Reynolds, John Scott Morgan, Justin Gainham, Linda McGregor, Natalie Barrington, Roger Carpenter, Terry Grealey and Victoria Carvey.

And last but not least, my parents, my girlfriend Candace for being patient with me and acting as my chauffeur, and a big thank you to the Tennant family for letting me use the house in Wiltshire.

Introduction

Wiltshire is known for many things: its little villages, old towns, ancient monuments and rolling hills, alternating with the flat plains that have led to its long-standing association with the military. All have combined to give it an interesting railway past. Who knows, for instance, that Stonehenge even had its own station at one point! Being situated in the south-west and crossing the Western and Southern Region boundaries, Wiltshire enjoyed service from the Great Western Railway (GWR) and the London and South Western Railway (L&SWR). If you drew a line across the county a third of the way up, it could be argued with few exceptions that the GWR got the top part, with Swindon at its heart, and the L&SWR got the bottom, with Salisbury as its centre. But, as road access to such places became easier, and as the military presence in the county shrank, so did the railway network. However, even after the Beeching cuts of the 1960s when whole lines and once-large stations disappeared, some of the little halts clung on and still survive. And, in fact, even today, a few of them continue to grow in a reversal of fortune.

When I was very young and standing on the platform of Falconwood station waiting to go to London, I announced that I wanted to be a train driver when I grew up. My oldest brother, Chris, informed me that it wasn't the job that it had once been and basically entailed moving a few levers and handles about, so there was little point. Whether or not this dissuaded me, I'm not sure, but before leaving school I decided to join the RAF instead. Failing to get enough GCSEs, I found myself taking the train crew exam at London Bridge station for the last place on that year's training course. I sat the test with one other candidate and though we both passed, he scored higher than I did so he won! In the end, I found myself in the book trade where I have been for many years, practising my love of books. Then, travelling down to Salisbury and Wiltshire by train to see my girlfriend and the family she worked for, I became interested in the railways of Wiltshire. It transpired that I had family connections with the county as well. One thing led to another and now I have written a book on the subject.

It would not be complete if it did not mention two special people in particular – the Poet Laureate and railway enthusiast John Betjeman who, as well as having a love of Wiltshire and the West Country, went to school at Marlborough, the railway history of which is uncovered in this volume; and, of course, the engineering genius and giant of his time, Isambard Kingdom Brunel, whose lasting legacy of the GWR Main Line through Wiltshire is also given due prominence.

Justin Bailey

1
Brunel in Wiltshire

The GWR Main Line from Swindon to Box

Swindon in the early 1960s, facing Paddington. (Lens of Sutton)

No book on the history of railways in Wiltshire could be complete without a chapter on Isambard Kingdom Brunel (1806–1859).

Brunel has been described as many things: 'the man who built the country', even 'the man who built the world'. Standing at little over five feet tall, he was a giant in a country that led the world in engineering. He designed and built everything from ships and the docks that held them, to railways and the tunnels, stations and bridges that they ran through and over. The son of a French engineer father, Sir Marc Brunel, he would go on to eclipse his father and, though many of his tunnels, bridges and stations still stand, his greatest legacy in Wiltshire is what some would call his finest achievement: the Great Western Railway and the main line route from Paddington in London to Bristol.

Brunel and his Broad Gauge

Brunel was appointed General Engineer of the Bristol Railway on 7th March 1833 and within a couple of days he was out surveying the land for a main line to link London with Bristol. At a meeting on 27th August to confirm his appointment, the Bristol Railway Company also took the step of changing its name to the now legendary 'Great Western Railway' (GWR).

Brunel had a clear-cut approach to railways, this being his first such project, and saw that it was vital to build the route as flat and as straight as possible. The London to Bristol main line, which received Royal Assent on 31st August 1835, was divided into five stretches that would ultimately be built as two larger sections. The entire route was surveyed by Brunel with help from his assistant, William Townsend, in the space of just nine weeks, often working twenty hours a day! And though Brunel was in charge, the two sections were built and managed as separate concerns by a variety of people.

The first section ran from London to Swindon, which was going to be the highest point on the line. It was mostly straight except for a few miles after Reading where the line ran north-east for a stretch before curving west again for

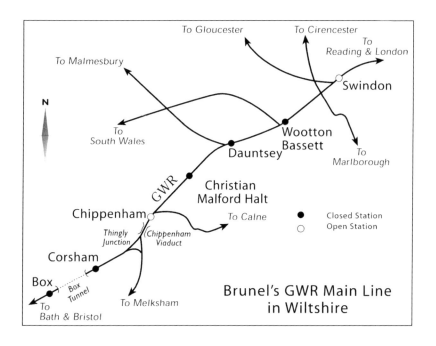

To Gloucester

To Cirencester

To Reading & London

To Malmesbury

N

Swindon

To South Wales

Wootton Bassett

Dauntsey

To Marlborough

GWR

Christian Malford Halt

Chippenham

To Calne

● Closed Station
○ Open Station

Thingly Junction

(Chippenham Viaduct)

Corsham

Box

Box Tunnel

To Melksham

To Bath & Bristol

Brunel's GWR Main Line in Wiltshire

Swindon. The second section from Swindon to Bristol, although helped by being downhill most of the way, was the more challenging. This direct and straight route was made possible only by the sheer amount of work that was carried out, in contrast to the first section. Deep cuttings were excavated, earthworks were constructed and bridges built over rivers. Tunnels were dug through the hills so the line didn't have to go over or around them, including the famous Box Tunnel. Except for the first 50 miles (graded at 1 in 1,320 feet) and two small stretches at Wootton Bassett and Box Tunnel (1 in 100 feet), the gradient of the line was less than 1 in 500 feet, a remarkable achievement for such a long route. It was nicknamed 'Brunel's billiards table' or 'Brunel's racetrack'.

Of course, this had a knock-on effect for many towns that were hoping that this new railway line might serve them – or were effectively isolated by it, like Marlborough (see Chapter 2) or Devizes (see Chapter 10). The armed forces also influenced railway development and eventually special lines, like the Bulford Branch Line (see Chapter 6), came to be built for them.

Brunel also considered that speed and the quality of the ride was of the essence in rail travel. Seemingly unimpressed with the 'standard gauge' of 4 ft 8½ ins between the rails used throughout the rest of the country (and most of the world) under the guidance of his contemporaries, especially George Stephenson, Brunel insisted that his broad gauge of 7 ft offered a more stable ride at higher speeds. His argument had a lot of merit and the GWR and other railway companies for which he acted as engineer laid 1,000 miles of broad gauge track. The matter came to a head when the GWR sought to expand into the Midlands in 1845, a move bitterly opposed by the railway companies there. Speed trials were run between broad gauge and standard gauge engines. The broad gauge engines won a convincing victory, but despite this Brunel lost out to what he saw as 'narrow gauge'! Too much of the country was standard gauge by then and, despite the GWR and Brunel fighting all the way, eventually all broad gauge tracks were converted, including his London to Bristol main line.

Before conversion, where the GWR and another company's line met in the same place, both gauges were in use together, as in Salisbury where the L&SWR standard gauge station and the GWR broad gauge station were next door to each other. In many cases a 'transfer shed' could be found where both gauges ran in and people and goods moved across the platform to the different gauged train on the other side. A very good example of broad gauge track, locomotive and transfer shed, can be seen today at Didcot Railway Centre next to Didcot station on Brunel's GWR main line, which is occasionally used on 'Steam Days'.

Swindon, the Railway Town

The journey on the Wiltshire portion of the GWR main line through the county should begin in Swindon. This was the spiritual as well as the industrial heart of the Great Western Railway.

The station itself is described in Chapter 6, but here a whole new part of the town grew up around its workshops. This was the 'Swindon Railway Village' or 'Swindon New Town' which, like the route, was designed by Brunel himself. In time, these workshops expanded to be amongst the largest locomotive and carriage works in the world. Swindon was chosen as it was at the summit of the route and though not exactly halfway, was near enough. It was the junction of the line to Gloucester and Cheltenham and was also served by the North Wiltshire and Wiltshire & Berkshire Canals. In a strange quirk, the canals and not the railway itself brought the coal to power the locomotives!

Brunel designed the early GWR broad gauge locomotives to very exacting specifications that seemed to be at odds with contemporary locomotive design. Though they had the very large driving wheel that later broad gauge engines retained, his locomotives turned out to be poor runners and unreliable. In 1837 the GWR employed Daniel Gooch, the brilliant Northern engineer, to head the Locomotive Department and become the man behind the Swindon Works. Though at first there was

Looking across part of the Swindon works. The main GWR Works Administration building is now owned by English Heritage. (Author)

tension between him and Brunel, they learned to respect each other.

The Swindon Works started operations in 1842 and, within a year, the workforce had risen to 423. By 1849 the factory consisted of an engine shed, a smithy, carpenters, boiler makers and various other shops and stores, covering approximately fourteen and a half acres. In 1846 the first locomotive to be built at Swindon, aptly named *Great Western*, left the Works, though it was not yet the powerhouse of railway industry that it became in later years.

In 1861 a mill was built to produce railway track but this closed in the 1870s when steel rail came into use and outside contractors could produce it more cheaply. In 1868

16

the complex expanded across the canal to a new wagon and carriage works. By 1873 new foundries were being built and by 1876 the workforce totalled 4,500. The early 1890s saw a boom in converting or scrapping broad gauge locomotives and stock, with 13 miles of sidings laid to store the now obsolete trains. Stock, including carriages, wagons and locomotives, could be converted in short order: on one occasion a party of directors from another railway company arriving by broad gauge watched their carriages converted while they waited, then boarded the same train and continued their journey!

Work continued at such a pace that men were drawn in from all around Swindon to make up the workforce. Swindon Works now employed more than 10,000 men and was one of the largest in the world. When a laundry was opened in 1892 it was washing 3,000,000 items a year! By 1901 the site had grown southwards and eastwards across the GWR main line to a fully-fledged locomotive works with larger boiler, body and erecting shops.

At the start of the 1900s a new erecting shop was opened which covered five and half acres and by 1919 this had been expanded to cover eleven and a half acres, almost the size of the whole original Works. To save space on the factory floor, all offices and toilets were built into the roof!

During the First World War the Works produced everything from artillery to ammunition, to parts for submarines. It held its centenary in 1935, when over 1,000 locomotives were repaired with two new ones being built every week. The Second World War once again saw the Works churning out everything from bombs, armour plate and parts for bridges and bombers to motorised landing craft. In the year of nationalisation (1948), the Works occupied no less than 326 acres, 77½ of them under cover.

Steam was its bread and butter and, as if to illustrate this, the last British Rail steam locomotive was built here, No.92220 *Evening Star* in March 1960.

After this the Western Region diesel hydraulic locomotives were built at Swindon. But by now the Works was in decline, and after the 'Main Workshops Future Plan' called for closure of half the railway workshops around the country, the Works was cut back progressively. Parts merged: the locomotive shop began to take on tasks that the carriage works used to do, after it closed in 1967, by which time the number of employees was down to around 6,000. By 1975 the site covered only 147 acres and in 1985 even the locomotive works was closed. Some minor work was still done at Swindon but complete closure followed in March 1986.

What Is Left Today

Much of the Swindon Works site, having been sold off to the council, has been cleared and redeveloped, though a few of the early and now listed buildings have been preserved. In June 2000 some of the remaining buildings were put to good use by becoming the site of 'Steam', the Museum of the Great Western Railway. Well worth visiting, it can be reached by one of the long tunnels that used to run under the Works. Coming out the other end you find yourself in the middle of what is left of the giant Works buildings, imposing in their stone grandeur. And though the old GWR offices, one of the most easily seen and recognised buildings in Swindon, is now used by English Heritage, some of the others are now only a façade. Other buildings around the old Works have been turned into shops and retail arcades.

The Swindon Works boiler shop is now a shopping arcade! (Author)

The old 'R' workshop is now the site of 'Steam, Museum of the Great Western Railway'. (Author)

The backyards of Brunel's Railway Village are all kept in good condition. (Author)

Brunel's Railway Village still stands and the homes and houses are used to this day. Well maintained and kept, to be among them is to step back in time. Looking like archetypal factory terraces, there are alleys between each block with a central entry and open brick-floored yard at the rear. A nice touch, perhaps added later, is an old wagon wheel set into the yard of every third house (or so). The large and imposing stone offices of the GWR Mechanics' Institute, on the other hand, have fared less well. At the time of writing the building is in a parlous state and has been fenced off and clad in scaffolding. Whether the work going on was to renovate or demolish it was unclear.

Swindon to Box Tunnel

Leaving Swindon, the line passed the connecting curve of Rushey Platt Junction that linked the main line to the M&SWJR, mentioned in Chapter 5. Passenger traffic ceased on this connection in 1961 although it continued to carry freight until 1970, including materials for the new M4 motorway. But after its other source of traffic, Moredon power station, closed, the line did as well and was lifted in 1978.

The first station on this stretch is Wootton Bassett. It opened in July 1841 but was rebuilt as Wootton Bassett Junction to cope with the new traffic for the South Wales line that opened on 1st January 1903. Two large platforms served up and down lines between them with the up platform having a bay at the down end for goods traffic. It closed to passengers in January 1965 and though freight had ceased a year earlier, coal traffic continued for ten months after the passenger closure date. Today, nothing remains of the station. However, this is not the end of Wootton Bassett's story. Due to the increasing size of the town population, North Wiltshire Council hoped to reopen it. In 2003 the Strategic Rail Authority refused to fund such a project, which led the council to remove the station from their 'wish list', but people are still hoping and if the land required is not sold off, there is still a chance of trains stopping at the town once more.

Leaving Wootton Bassett, the line passed through an expanse of passing loops and sidings before travelling straight on or branching off to the right for the South Wales line. All that is left of these sidings now is an up loop line and a couple of sidings parallel to the down line serving a Foster Yeoman stone terminal.

The next station on the main line is Dauntsey, mentioned

GWR Hall Class *crossing the Western Arches, Chippenham, in 1952.* (*Millbrook House Ltd*)

in Chapter 11 as the original starting point for the Malmesbury Branch. Christian Malford Halt came next, a very basic affair with short up and down platforms that lasted from 1926 to 1965. Chippenham, as detailed in Chapter 10, was the junction for the Calne Branch.

West of Chippenham station are the monumental Western Arches. Built in Bath stone, with one main span of 26 ft flanked by two smaller spans of 10 ft, it towers over the junction of the A4 and A420. This is followed by the six-arch Chippenham Viaduct, again built in Bath stone, which still spans the A420 in all its Brunelian glory.

Next we arrive at Thingley Junction, where the line divides once again but this time to the left and the Westbury route via Melksham and the main line to Weymouth. From 1943 to 1955 there was a third side to this junction to make a triangle. Thingley Junction is also home to a network of sidings to the right of the down line. These were opened in the Second World War for the marshalling of ammunition that was stored in the area, especially around Corsham and in the quarries of Box Tunnel. After the war, traffic here decreased and some sidings were taken up. The site however was bought from the Ministry of Defence by Rail and Marine Engineering in 1995 and put by them to good use following the Hatfield rail crash in 2001. This led to a major track renewal programme and the sidings were used for welding new track into 240 ft lengths to make CWS (Continuous Welded Rail).

The last station before Box Tunnel was Corsham. This was a substantial conventional station with up and down platforms either side of the tracks and a very large Station Hotel towering over the up platform. It was limited in its size, however, because it was set in a cutting. Originally opening in June 1841, it closed to passengers on the same day as Wootton Bassett, 4th January 1965, when the local passenger service between Bristol and Swindon was axed.

Freight, however, was the major traffic from Corsham, especially stone from the nearby mines and from the underground quarries of Box Tunnel. By 1864 100,000 tons of stone blocks were leaving Corsham every year. These were marshalled in freight sidings just west of the station which were adjacent to and all but part of the 2 ft 6 in narrow gauge railway used to transfer the stone from the mines and quarries. This narrow gauge network closed in 1939, after the station had suffered a lean period between the wars as passenger levels saw a steady decline. Though stone still continued to be loaded for rail here, the goods service ceased in June 1963. Private sidings and a loading dock still carried on but these have since gone as well. The

Swindon to Bristol pick-up freight at Corsham, 1951. (Millbrook House Ltd)

only remnant of the station now is the large goods shed used as a garage by Lineside. As at Wootton Bassett, there were plans for a new station at Corsham but, again, these have yet to be realised.

Box Tunnel and the Corsham Quarries

After Corsham it is only a small distance to that other monument of Brunel's railway, Box Tunnel. This proved to be the most challenging project as well. At 9,636 ft long (almost two miles), in its day it was a magnificent feat of engineering and perhaps typical of the way that Brunel wanted this main line built. Why go around or over a hill, like Box Hill, when you can go through it? Its planning caused great concern and alarm among sceptics, onlookers and other interested parties and was enough to promote many scare stories. Oxygen starvation deep within the tunnel was one. Train brake failure on the 1 in 100 gradient (the steepest on the whole line) that might lead to speeds of more than 120mph and certain death, was another!

To begin the work in 1837 a series of shafts were sunk, 25 ft in diameter and ranging from 70 to 300 ft deep. Many contractors balked at the prospect of such a job but eventually teams were found to carry out the work in two halves. George Burge from Herne Bay tackled the western end and a local team of Lewis and Brewer did the eastern, with work proper beginning in 1838. The tunnel is 39 ft high by 35 ft wide and over three years 414,000 cubic yards of material was excavated through solid rock. Conditions were horrific and in a rush to get the tunnel finished as soon as possible the workforce grew to 4,000 men. A ton

The magnificent west portal of Brunel's masterpiece that is Box Tunnel. It is almost 2 miles long and 300 ft underground at its deepest point. (Author)

each of gunpowder and candles were being used every week and, by the tunnel's opening on 30th June 1841, it had claimed the lives of over 100 men.

It is perhaps the tunnel portals that give the most impressive sight. The grand west portal extends into a shallow cutting and the portal face is built beautifully in carved Bath stone: the main cornice is set on curved stone corbels with a stone balustrade along the top. Such craftsmanship would not look out of place on the front of a grand country house. In the middle, yawning, is the tall pitch-black tunnel mouth like an entrance to the underworld! This can be seen from the A4, which crosses the line near the front of the tunnel. A little viewing gallery has been built before the bridge is crossed, complete with a plaque set in stone that gives facts about the tunnel. The east portal, however, set deep in a dark sheer-faced cutting, is nowhere near as grand. This portal has been reinforced and lined with extra brick, bringing it somewhat lower than the western one, nearer to standard gauge height. This extra brick lining also spoils the appearance to a large degree.

The actual tunnel was mainly, and perhaps surprisingly, unlined, leaving a ceiling and walls of bare rock protected in parts by a wooden roof. There were so many rock falls from the ceiling in the early days that more and more of it has been lined since.

To the right of the east portal is another smaller tunnel which is part of one of the tales surrounding Box Tunnel. This used to be the entrance to Box Tunnel Quarry and led deep inside Box Hill. When the main rail tunnel was being excavated such good quality stone was encountered that it began to be quarried on a commercial basis and Tunnel Quarry to the north was opened in 1844. By 1862, five miles of narrow gauge railway extended from this entrance under Box Hill and Corsham Downs.

Originally a broad gauge siding ran into this tunnel from the main line but when the main line converted to standard gauge, the extra room in the cutting allowed this siding to be run as a separate line all the way to Corsham. The height of this minor tunnel was also increased to take standard gauge box vans. Mining in the underground quarry ceased in 1930, but then it was taken over by the War Department to store ammunition. A new platform and loading/unloading facility was built inside the tunnel and up to 2,000 tons of ammunition could be moved every

day by a small fleet of standard gauge diesel shunters.
Adapted to work underground, they were kept here
for use on munition trains. The conversion from stone
quarry to what was one of the largest munition storage
bunkers in the country ran wildly over budget and worse
was to come!

In 1940 the quarry south-east of Box Tunnel, Spring
Quarry, was earmarked for use as an underground aircraft
engine factory by the Bristol Aircraft Company after Lord
Beaverbrook put pressure on Winston Churchill to protect
aircraft production from German bombing. What followed
was the creation of a massive white elephant. Regardless of
the fact that the Bristol Aircraft Company and its staff did
not want to move underground, preferring to take their
chances 'up above', work was started on the largest
underground factory in the world. The figures are
staggering: 2,200,000 square feet were divided into three
sections not by man, but instead by the geological faults
under Box Hill!

To help get the 20,000 workers in and out, escalators were
'poached' from various London Underground stations
including St Paul's and Holborn. No less than five canteens
could cater for 6,000 people at one sitting. When the factory
was closed in 1945 after the anticipated German attacks on
it never materialised, the total cost was a staggering
£20,000,000! All that there was to show for this was a small
number of aircraft engines that reportedly failed at test
because of the assembly conditions in the factory where
they were built!

After the Second World War much of the site of Spring
Quarry was used for storage. In April 1954, the quarry
freehold was bought from the Bath and Portland Stone
Company by the government. It was then converted once
more, at further expense, to be suitable as an Emergency

Government War Headquarters (EGWHQ) in the event of a nuclear war. Once again, Holborn Underground station gave up its escalators to help in the building of this new bunker, now code-named 'Subterfuge'. The accommodation was built to take 7,700 staff and the communications facilities were state of the art. It should be remembered that the railway tunnel that ran through all of this, though sealed off from it by thick walls, still continued to be used! By 1959 the work was nearly complete but had slowed as the defence budget was cut back, and the RAF, having experience of working in the quarries around Corsham, was given the job of getting the project done. By the Cuban missile crisis of 1962 the Chiefs of Staff were asking when it would be finished in case they had to take up rooms in what was now code-named 'Burlington'.

After the Cuban crisis the site was left to deteriorate and in the late 1960s the code-name changed again, to 'Turnstile'. Succeeding governments have updated the site in parts but it is now outdated: though 80 to 100 ft below ground, this is not secure against modern nuclear weapons. The rock falls that plagued the railway tunnel in its early days still plagued the quarries and the name given to 'Spring Quarry' gave a hint to the fact that it was never completely waterproof either! It became a shadow of what it once was and today the whole area is still owned by the Ministry of Defence. Though they remain tight-lipped about what now goes on there, theories abound, including it being a storage place for UFOs! All ammunition was removed from Tunnel Quarry and the railway line into it was taken out of use between 1973 and 1974 with the entrance secured against intruders, though it can still be seen while passing by.

However, two great myths about Box Tunnel persist. The first is that huge emergency stocks of steam locomotives are

Box station in 1951. (P J Garland Collection)

secretly hidden deep in the tunnel in case of a war, nuclear or otherwise. Often known as the 'Strategic Reserve', some people still intent on finding this steam treasure enter the tunnel in search of it! Of course this is foolhardy as it's a busy high speed line. Not too long ago intruders trying to find this greatest of railway Holy Grails were escorted out of the tunnel by police and were soon seen in court. The second and perhaps best-known myth is that Brunel laid out the tunnel so that the sun can shine through the length of it on one day each year, 9th April, his birthday! However, taking into account refraction and the effect of the earth's atmosphere, in 1988 BR engineers calculated this to be possible only on 6th and 7th April!

Box Tunnel to North East Somerset

Leaving Box Tunnel westwards, the line travels under a road bridge and passes two sidings, once again used for loading stone. These are situated just before a small stop that became known as Box (Mill Lane). Though it was just a halt, it was not named as such. This stop opened in March 1930 and lasted until 4th January 1965. Interestingly, it is nearer to the village of Box than Box station is!

Trains then enter the 198-yard-long Middle Hill Tunnel, which though a lot shorter than Box Tunnel, also has portals that are great works of stone craftsmanship in a Roman style.

The last station before the border with North East Somerset is Box, located outside the western portal of Middle Hill Tunnel. Opened on 30th June 1841, the station buildings were in Brunel's chalet style, and a side platform and an island platform served three through-running tracks with a number of sidings. The island platform was fenced on one side so as to present only one face to passenger trains. The tracks running behind it served a loop, which was all part of a small goods yard that included an area with cranes for loading stone. One goods shed and an engine shed, along with the quirkily named Box Signal Box, completed the station. Freight was carried until June 1963 and Box station closed on the now-familiar 4th January 1965. Nothing is left of it, as vegetation has overtaken the whole site.

2
The Midland & South Western Junction Railway: 1

Swindon Town to Savernake Low Level via Marlborough Low Level including Marlborough High Level

The history of the Midland & South Western Junction Railway (M&SWJR) is, perhaps above all else, a tale of triumph over adversity.

The story begins as far back as 1846, but construction of the M&SWJR proper started in 1875, only to cease in 1878 when the company went bankrupt. Work restarted in 1879 and the railway finally opened in 1881. Not so much a single railway to begin with, it was more a collection of railways that joined each other. These included the Swindon, Marlborough and Andover Railway (SM&AR), the Swindon and Cheltenham Extension Railway (S&CER) and the Marlborough and Grafton Railway (M&GR); all built in different places at different times.

In its entirety, it was to become the M&SWJR in its own right in 1884 with the amalgamation of the SM&AR and the S&CER, continually fighting against and eventually overcoming the pressures of the Great Western Railway (GWR) which, it seems, did everything it could to stop the railway being built. For 48 years it enjoyed a fraught but

Trackbed of the former M&SWJR outside Marlborough. (Author)

well-loved existence, until 1923 when, in a final act of irony and supreme insult, it was taken over by the GWR, before finally closing in 1961. Its loss is still felt today.

While the complete route ran from Cheltenham to Andover, the bulk of the line ran through Wiltshire, from Cricklade to Ludgershall. The first section to be built, and the focus of this chapter, was from Swindon to Savernake via Marlborough.

In the Beginning

The railway mania of the Victorian era reached its climax in the mid-1800s. Indeed, Christopher Awdry's *Encyclopaedia of British Railway Companies* (PSL, 1990) records the history of no less than 1,000 separate railway companies in the U.K. – a far cry from the mere dozen we have today! It was in those heady days that the M&SWJR was born; a collection of two or three railway companies that eventually became one.

It began in 1846 when a Bill was put before Parliament to allow the Manchester and Southampton Railway to run from the Birmingham and Gloucester line, about a mile and a half from Cheltenham, to the south coast port of Southampton. This 88-mile route, planned by Robert Stephenson and the engineer George Bidder, would run through the Cotswolds via Cirencester, into the Vale of the White Horse at Cricklade, then east of Swindon through the Marlborough Downs, Marlborough itself, onwards to Savernake Forest and then fringing Salisbury Plain south of Andover. From here it would go down to Southampton. This would have been no mean feat as it would have entailed viaducts, earthworks and lengthy tunnels – about four miles of tunnel in all. The cost would have been an astronomical £1,500,000. The Midland Railway would have contributed the sum of £400,000 but the rest would have had to be raised by other means.

The appeal of this route was that while on the one hand, the area it would travel through was sparsely populated, on the other, a link between the Midlands and the south coast was very appealing, especially to the industries so prevalent in the Midlands at the time. It would not be just any railway link. The 'ace up the sleeve' of Messrs Stephenson and Bidder was that this would be a standard gauge link through territory which, owned by the GWR at that time, was very much broad gauge (7 feet). While Brunel's Great Western broad gauge did have its merits, it was incompatible with the standard gauge railways spreading so quickly throughout the rest of the country.

So, above all else, a north–south railway route without a break of gauge or trains was what was used to try and sell the route. Of course, the Great Western was not going to ignore a competitor passing through its territory and lobbied against it intensely. Even so, such an attractive proposition as this was hard to turn down and the bill passed the House of Commons and nearly made it through the House of Lords as well. It was only defeated by the casting vote of the chairman in the House of Lords' committee, and even then, only after the GWR had made the concession of converting the route between Oxford and Basingstoke to mixed gauge. So while the north–south standard gauge route was in a very roundabout way now open, it still left the centre of Wiltshire isolated and cut off from any standard gauge routes.

A second, rival project called 'The Manchester, Southampton and Poole Railway' was put forward. This route was much the same as Stephenson and Bidder's but south of Marlborough it was going to run to Salisbury before going on to link up with the London & South

Western Railway (L&SWR) via a new branch line at Bishopstoke (Eastleigh) on the London to Southampton line. Then it would continue through Fordingbridge to the Southampton and Dorchester Railway. This route was promoted by Charles Henry Lacey of Kenyon House, Manchester, with Joseph Locke as his engineer. This scheme however, did not progress far in Parliament. Then in 1847 a modified version of the Manchester and Southampton scheme was brought forward. But with the concession by the GWR now on the books, even this modified plan died an early death.

The Marlborough Connection

With the death of the prospective Manchester and Southampton Railway, towns in central Wiltshire, it seemed, were once again condemned to isolation. Marlborough had perhaps more cause than most to feel aggrieved. Not only was it a big town but it also had one of the most famous schools in the country. But, with no rail connection, residents and the boys at the College (or Marlburians as they are also known), had to reach it by crossing the Marlborough Downs in a horse-drawn bus from Swindon station. As one can imagine, not something that was relished in the winter!

So although the earlier projects passed into history, efforts to reach Marlborough by rail did not. The GWR was troubled for many years by schemes and ideas that all came to nothing, but gradually the original plan got off the ground; unfortunately, though, only the parts south of Andover! In 1858, the Andover and Redbridge Railway (A&RR) linked Andover with Southampton, then was swallowed up by the L&SWR in 1863. An attempt was made to extend northwards to Savernake but this was unsuccessful. The high rolling plateau, which stands between the Vale of Pewsey and the Kennet Valley at Marlborough, was an obstruction to any northward expansion. However, in July 1861, the Marlborough Railway Act authorised the GWR to bridge this obstacle with a 5½-mile extension from the Berkshire and Hampshire Extension Railway station at Savernake (worked by the GWR) to a new GWR station at Marlborough.

At last, Marlborough had a rail link, known variously as the Marlborough Railway or the Marlborough Extension. But it was broad gauge, and steeply graded at that. By 1874, however, the writing was on the wall for broad gauge in the area and this line, like many others around it, was converted to standard gauge.

The line branched off from the Berkshire and Hampshire route and ran single-track to the Marlborough GWR station, which in 1924 would become Marlborough High Level station. The Swindon, Marlborough & Andover Railway (SM&AR – see below) would begin by running over the GWR line using Marlborough South Junction to make the link to Savernake. However, being owned by the GWR this most important link would be a major thorn in the side of the SM&AR.

In 1898 the Marlborough and Grafton Railway (M&GR), a sister company set up for the purpose by the M&SWJR, built its own separate line from Marlborough to Savernake which naturally began to affect traffic on the GWR's Marlborough line though the GWR station remained open for passengers until 6th March, 1933, some ten years after the M&SWJR had been absorbed by the GWR. By that time, Marlborough High Level station was closed, though its goods yard was still used for a while after.

A Main Line at Last!

While the GWR extension to Marlborough was a start, for the people of Wiltshire it was not enough. In May 1872, prominent citizens and business people from the area met in the Forest Hotel in Savernake. There, an engineer from London, John Sewell, put forward his plans for a new railway, namely the Swindon, Marlborough, Southampton and New Forest Railway.

The meeting resulted in a new company being formed, with a modified prospectus for the railway. A bill went before Parliament in 1873 for capital of £375,000 with powers to borrow £125,000 more. To raise the parliamentary deposit took some difficulty but the irony was that since Parliament thought the scheme, like the others before it, had little chance of succeeding, opposition was thin on the ground and the bill was actually passed with little difficulty! On 21st July 1873 the Swindon, Marlborough and Andover Railway Act received Royal Assent.

This new railway was to be built in two major sections: the first from Swindon to Marlborough and the second from Wolfall Junction near Savernake to a site 1½ miles from Andover Junction station just across the border in Hampshire. In between the two sections and linking them was the GWR's Marlborough Extension, which itself was to be rebuilt with a shallower gradient. Rather oddly, there was an agreement that this section of the SM&AR would not actually join the L&SWR line at Andover. Instead, a third line was to be built linking the two, owned by the L&SWR but leased to the SM&AR.

The Building of the Line

On 28th July, 1875, the M.P. for Marlborough and the first chairman of the company, Lord Ernest Brudenell-Bruce, turned the first sod of the new line at an inauguration ceremony in Swindon. Unfortunately, by this time, only £6,000 of the £400,000 needed had been raised. Notwithstanding this, a contract was given to William Wright for the building of the line but even before much progress had been made, the money ran out and, with no wages being paid, work stopped in 1876. To make matters worse, the work that had been done was of such poor quality that the structures collapsed.

Two years later, a new start was made, with one of the most loyal proponents of the SM&AR being the bursar of Marlborough College, J. S. Thomas, who along with the Solicitor of the line, J. C. Townsend, kept faith with the company to avoid it becoming extinct. So, in 1879, a new contractor, Messrs Watson, Smith and Watson, began the task of building the line, though this time with modified plans to reduce costs. These included a different starting point in Swindon, replacing the tunnel with a gradient north to Rushey Platt. At Chiseldon and Marlborough, curves and embankments would replace expensive viaducts. Ironically it was these money-saving deviations from the original plan that were to give the SM&AR and then the M&SWJR its character and quirkiness.

With new hope and enthusiasm, building went ahead rapidly and the Swindon to Marlborough section was officially opened on 28th July 1881. The first paying passengers were carried the day before, amongst them 80 boys from Marlborough College on their journey home.

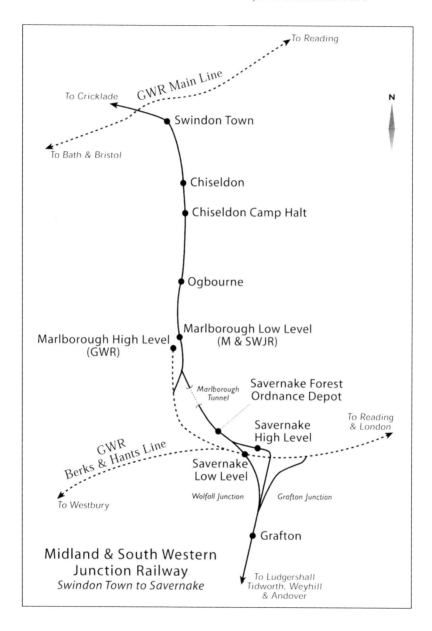

The Line in Detail

The 'new' Swindon Town station was built on rather a tight curve within a narrow cutting but despite this, room was made for many sidings, a turntable, engine shed and a goods shed. Originally three tracks ran between two platforms but as time went by remodelling took place and one side and one island platform served two tracks one side and three the other. The general offices of the SM&AR were also located in a large elegant building overlooking the station. It closed in 1924 but fortunately the building survives.

Heading south to Chiseldon the single line ran onto high chalkland but like Swindon, Chiseldon was in a valley and was situated in a cutting. Though the station was not that large it had three sidings and, as well as a good quantity of local traffic, especially from Swindon, steady revenue came in from transporting racehorses for the nearby training stables. The line was double through the station and for a little way after it. However, the right-hand line was in fact not much more than a long siding serving what was then Draycott Camp. Later this line was to become part of the GWR and its name changed to Chiseldon Camp Halt.

Further on came Ogbourne, one of the smallest stations on the line. The track again ran double through the station, which had two sidings. At one time another long, private siding/passing loop was used for stables 1½ miles down the line at Ogbourne St Andrew. This was owned by a Major Edwards who had his own horsebox.

The next station was Marlborough. Opened in 1881, it was one of the main, if not the major, reasons why the line was built at all. Marlborough was also one of the most curious stations on the line. Built on a sharp curve, the SM&AR station with double tracks was located a mere

The site of the former Swindon Town station with the old M&SJWR office building in the centre background. (Author)

stone's throw from the GWR station with its own Marlborough extension. Five sidings, with a very large goods shed, branched off from the curve before the platforms were reached. The ends of these sidings met an approach road to the station and beyond this was the Andover to Marlborough road, which ran through a cutting under the main line. As Marlborough was a market town the station was quite big to cope with the expected trade. The SM&AR line crossed the Andover to Marlborough road with a loading platform and siding on the left. For a brief spell, this is where the line ended. But in 1883 the line was extended, still double, before running parallel to the GWR station. It joined the GWR line a little further on at Marlborough South Junction. It would now run over the GWR Marlborough Extension. But here the trouble began...

Swindon Town station in 1955 with a Cheltenham to Southampton train. (Milepost 92½)

The GWR Digs In!

Back in 1873 when the prospect of the SM&AR and a north–south link through Wiltshire looked very unlikely, the GWR was content to rest on its laurels; even more so when the SM&AR went bankrupt just as soon as it had begun. But by 1881, the GWR began to realise it was going to have a fight on its hands. There would be no love lost between these two companies, especially when the SM&AR became friends with the L&SWR, a major enemy of the GWR in this part of the country.

While the SM&AR had built a competitive route in theory, in practice it still had to make it all work as one line, including the anticipated section from Swindon, north to Cheltenham. The GWR still held the aces in the guise of two critical locations on this route where the SM&AR was forced, for the time being, to run its trains over GWR tracks. The GWR employed suspect business practices, underhand means and dirty tricks to make sure its new neighbour and competitor suffered. The two locations in question were Rushey Platt Junction, just north of Swindon, and the section from Marlborough to Wolfall Junction just south of Savernake.

With the SM&AR being in no great financial state, the GWR saw this as a chance to 'put the boot in' and levied extortionate tolls for the use of its tracks. While these were reduced at arbitration it was still money that the SM&AR could ill afford.

The Marlborough Extension was barely fit for GWR traffic, let alone anyone else's, and Board of Trade inspectors demanded major improvements to be made in signalling on the line and at Savernake station before it could be jointly used by the SM&AR. Of course, the GWR was in no hurry to see this work carried out and when it was finally completed, it was the SM&AR that had to pay for it! The improvements were finished in January 1883 at the same time that arbitration brought to an end the disputes between the two companies over the use of the GWR facilities. So, on 5th February, the SM&AR opened for business between Swindon and Andover, nearly ten years after the company had been set up. The cost was over £600,000 and, on top of that, the northern extension to Cheltenham was about to begin as well.

However, if people thought that things would now settle down between the SM&AR and GWR, they were much mistaken. One of the conditions of being able to use the GWR Marlborough Extension was that the SM&AR was not allowed to carry local traffic, that is, passengers between Marlborough and Wolfall Junction and vice versa. Anyone wishing to use the SM&AR had to obtain a ticket for a station further up or down the line. To make sure that these conditions were adhered to, GWR ticket inspectors would insist on checking tickets on all trains, taking as much time as they wished! In the first years of service, the GWR thought nothing of delaying a SM&AR train, on one occasion for five hours! All this, of course, dragged the SM&AR ever more deeply into debt and trouble.

Savernake Station to Wolfall Junction

The GWR Savernake station, or Savernake Low Level as it was to become, was the last stop on the SM&AR for this section of the line. After it, came Wolfall Junction, which led to Grafton station and the beginning of the second section of what was to become the M&SWJR. Savernake was the station that caused most trouble between the GWR and SM&AR.

Originally the starting point of the GWR Marlborough Extension, Savernake began life as a single-platform affair serving a passing loop. It had two sidings for local goods and freight. When the Marlborough Extension opened, the platform was converted to have a bay at the 'up' end to serve Extension traffic. From here it ran as a double line for shunting purposes before it became the single line to Marlborough.

When Major Marindin inspected the line on 21st March 1882, on a special train in very unpleasant weather, he expressed great misgivings about Savernake station and its ability to serve both railway companies. Improvements would have to be made: carried out by the GWR but paid for by the SM&AR. This caused problems with the SM&AR so they opened the Grafton to Andover section and ran a horse omnibus service between Marlborough and Grafton. Eventually the improvements were made, including a new platform on the down line of the Berks and Hants Railway (to be used as an 'up' platform on the Marlborough line) and a new siding just before the new platform.

After more wrangling and arbitration, the SM&AR finally ran through trains from Swindon to Andover on 5th February 1883. Beyond Savernake station, a little way along the GWR Berks and Hants line, at Wolfall Junction the SM&AR branched off to continue its route to Grafton and on to Andover.

The End and What is Left Today

The repercussions of closing the M&SWJR can still be felt today, with towns like Cirencester and Marlborough having no railway link. It is ironic since Cirencester and Marlborough had two stations each at one time! However, even when all sections of the line were finally linked and amalgamation by the three main railway companies of the three main sections took place in 1884, the line still did not attract the desired passenger numbers. The difficult relationship with the GWR and the early plight of its parlous finances saw the M&SWJR struggling more often than not. With so many compromises made in its early construction to save money, it missed the chance of being properly integrated with the lines around it. Military traffic resulting from the Boer War and the First World War was the only reason it did as well as it did.

In 1921 the big four (the L&SWR, the GWR, the LMS and the LNER) swallowed up many separate and individual lines across the country. While the M&SWJR survived at first, being so deep in its enemy's territory meant it was not long before it was taken over by the GWR. This brought rationalisation and, while some cost-cutting was done, double lines becoming single and stations closed, money was put into the line as well. Some parts of the route saw improved service and sections of the line were strengthened to take the heavier GWR locomotives. A couple of new stations were opened (though these were just halts), namely Chiseldon Camp and Collingbourne Kingston.

In the Second World War, the line again experienced an upsurge of military traffic. But after that it fell once again into decline and piece by piece the route and its stations

Approach road to Marlborough Low Level station site, now the drive to Kennet District Council works yard. (Author)

were closed. By 1959, two years before the closure of the complete line, the section through Savernake High Level (see Chapter 4) to Grafton South Junction was closed, routing trains through Savernake Low Level. The last train ran on 13th September 1958 and after this a rail was taken up on the bridge over the Kennet and Avon Canal.

The route of the M&SWJR is fortunate, however, to still have a good deal of its track bed to walk or cycle on. Looking at any OS Explorer map of this area you will see it plainly marked. The site of Swindon Town station is now an industrial park but a key building, the old M&SWJR general offices, still exists in perfect condition and below this, on the cutting wall, can be seen a mural

Bridge abutment that carried the M&SJWR over what is now the A346 outside Marlborough Low Level station. (Author)

depicting the railway history of the site. Walking under Devizes Road Bridge, a public bridlepath carries on to Rushey Platt on the old track bed. At Marlborough the track bed can be walked around the town, as it has become a public bridleway.

From Froxfield the A4 goes over the section that leaves Marlborough for Ogbourne St Andrew and Chiseldon. The site of Marlborough Low Level station is now owned by Kennet District Council and used as a yard for their road and maintenance vehicles so is not open to the public. However, the station approach road, with its stone-clad sides, is used to reach the yard and can still be seen through the gates. A little way past this you can still see the bridge abutments that carried the line over what was once the A338 but is now the A346. With so much in evidence, there is plenty more to explore if one has the time!

Marlborough and the John Betjeman Connection

Probably one of Marlborough College's best-known pupils was Sir John Betjeman, the Poet Laureate between 1972 and 1984. He attended Marlborough College from 1920 to 1925 and during this time was not averse to cycling to Swindon to look at the trains.

The down platform of Dilton Marsh Halt on the Salisbury to Westbury line. The plaque bearing John Betjeman's poem is the small sign on the side of the waiting room. (Author)

The plaque showing Sir John Betjeman's poem. (Author)

While his love for the West Country seems to imply that he was a GWR man at heart, some of his more famous poems would dictate otherwise. *Metropolitan Railway, Harrow on the Hill* and *Middlesex* were about his fascination with the early days of Southern Electric, the London Underground and transport in London and its suburbs. However, in his poem *Dilton Marsh Halt*, written in the early 1970s about a little station on the Westbury to Salisbury line, he champions its survival against all the odds and repeated attempts to close it. When its future was finally assured after being refurbished and reopened in 1994 (ten years after the passing of Sir John), his daughter Candida Lycett Green unveiled a plaque at the little station commemorating it. Today Dilton Marsh Halt can be reached by rail from Swindon, Salisbury and Westbury. If you wish to alight at it you have to ask the conductor to stop the train, and if you wish to catch a train from there you have to hail it as if asking a bus to stop!

After a career in literature, books on architecture and some early TV documentaries, including one on Marlborough where he took a backward look at the College, Sir John Betjeman's last public appearance, rather fittingly, was at St Pancras station on 24th June 1983. Here he unveiled a plaque on BR Main Line Electric Locomotive 86229, named in his honour *Sir John Betjeman*. Tickets to ride the train hauled by the locomotive that day to Bedford and back cost a mere £10. One wonders what the great man would make of things now.

3
The Midland & South Western Junction Railway: 2

Grafton Junction to Ludgershall and Tidworth/Tidworth Barracks

The second part of our trip down the M&SWJR takes us from the complex Grafton Junction to Ludgershall on the edge of Hampshire, then off the M&SWJR, along the branch line to Tidworth and Tidworth Barracks which was built especially for the military.

Grafton Junction to Ludgershall

Grafton Junction was a major junction on the M&SWJR. It was called the Berkshire and Hampshire Line and can best be described as a downward pointing triangle: the bottom point on Andover (M&SWJR) and the line across the top being the GWR Reading–Devizes–Westbury line.

The right side of the triangle was known as the Grafton Curve and was built mainly for military traffic and the odd excursion. The left side of the triangle was the M&SWJR to Savernake, Marlborough and onwards to Swindon. Though there was a level link joining this 'west' side to the GWR line at Wolfall Junction, halfway up the left side of the triangle it divided and the main M&SWJR crossed the GWR line over a bridge. At this point both lines ran more or less parallel to Savernake in the west, if at a different elevation to each other.

Running very close alongside the GWR line that formed the top of the triangle was the Kennet and Avon Canal. This canal was well used between Reading and Bristol from 1810 but fell into decline as the railways moved into the area. It was bought by the GWR in 1857.

After leaving Grafton Junction, the first station was Grafton and Burbage, commonly shortened to 'Grafton'. It was built by John Dover and opened on 1st May 1882. In 1902 a two-mile line was opened to Dodsdown, in the north-east, and a brickworks owned by A.J. Keeble of Peterborough who operated the line to supply material for the contractors building Tidworth barracks. Although the line closed in 1910, so much traffic was conveyed in its existence that three sidings were built where it joined the M&SWJR just to the north of the station. These also served as a collecting point for other freight traffic bound for Tidworth barracks.

Grafton station was a pretty bleak place by all accounts. It served the villages of Grafton and Burbage, which were 1½ miles away in a sparsely populated area. Some accounts speak of wildlife roaming freely over the platforms and the rabbit population caused such mayhem by burrowing into the embankments that they had to be gassed out. When the weather turned bad the station usually caught the full force of it. It was struck by lightning on 21st August 1925 and severely damaged.

Moving down the line towards Salisbury Plain we come to Collingbourne Kingston Halt. Built by the GWR when the line became part of their network, it was a minor affair serving the village, with platforms constructed of railway sleepers. A little further on, serving the village of Collingbourne Ducis was Collingbourne station, with two platforms and a little siding for a horse dock. Unlike Grafton it was situated right next to the village. It originally had a signal box that was notable for its height, but that was its undoing when the bottom timbers were found to be unsafe and in the rebuilding it was lowered and redesigned.

In 1888, plans were put forward for a little branch line, approximately 7 miles long, to run from Collingbourne to Fittleton. To be called the Collingbourne and Avon Railway, it had the backing of three landowners: Sir Michael Edward Hicks Beach, who was President of the Board of Trade and Lord of the Manor of Fittleton; Sir John Dugdale Astley and his trustees; and the Marquis of Ailsbury and his trustees. A track plan had the line running parallel to the M&SWJR line for about 800 yards in the direction of Ludgershall. However, the scheme came to nothing.

It was not far to Ludgershall from Collingbourne, about half the distance from Grafton to Collingbourne. At its inception as part of the SM&AR (Southern Section) in 1882, Ludgershall was a simple station, with two tracks serving two platforms and a small goods shed and yard. In 1900, however, things began to change. The army had grand designs for Salisbury Plain and the War Office decided to build barracks and a garrison at nearby Tidworth, to be served by a branch line from Ludgershall, which became an important junction and expanded to become one of the biggest stations on the M&SWJR. A hotel was built there called the Prince of Wales and by 1902 the station had been remodelled and rebuilt.

The platforms, typical of stations built or adapted for military purposes, were very large. Covered in gravel to provide a better surface for the thousands of soldiers and horses passing through, they needed a lot of hoeing to keep them tidy and kept the station staff constantly busy!

By 1923 the station area covered 16 acres. Two lines ran through the station, with very wide platforms either side. These were so big that two sidings ran into and all but through them, in effect creating another two platforms either side of these. About halfway down, a footbridge linked all the platforms. With a corrugated-iron roof covering its entire length, three staircases down to platform level and sides of a lattice-girder construction, it would not have looked out of place on a model railway! The booking office was quite substantial and beyond and to the south, passing under a road bridge at the neck of the station, lay a goods yard, with a loading platform over 600 ft long. Along with this were eleven sidings serving an engine shed, a turntable, a goods shed and a coal stage.

On 8th November 1917, during the First World War, King George V arrived at Ludgershall on the Royal Train to

Ludgershall station, Andover direction, in 1958. (P J Garland Collection)

Ludgershall station, Cheltenham direction, in 1948. (P J Garland Collection)

inspect the troops; his horses were conveyed by L&SWR horsebox. He stayed for three days and troops assembled at the station, outside the booking office, to form a King's Guard. Needless to say, everyone turned out in their best finery, with a good contingent from the local constabulary.

The Tidworth Barracks Branch

The branch line from Ludgershall to the military base at Tidworth was built by a Mr Lovatt on land owned by the War Department but was operated by the M&SWJR. It left the M&SWJR just past the road bridge mentioned above and before Ludgershall goods yard. Though beginning as a double, past the sidings the track soon became single. The

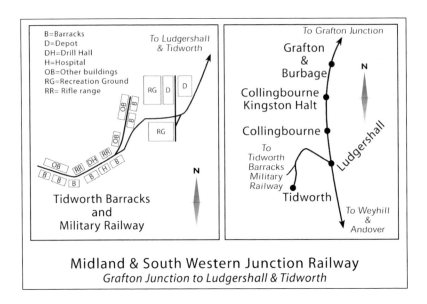

Midland & South Western Junction Railway
Grafton Junction to Ludgershall & Tidworth

line climbed Tidworth Down where a major engineering project was carried out so it could travel through a steeply-sided chalk cutting. In 1901, the line opened for use by the army, with goods and passenger traffic following in 1902. By this time the branch had five lines, two ending at a bay platform while the remaining three carried on for a short distance.

The first two-thirds of Tidworth station's platforms were in Wiltshire with the last third in Hampshire! On the M&SWJR only Swindon Town and Ludgershall stations were bigger than Tidworth, and the Tidworth stationmaster was senior to all his colleagues. Receipts were greater than for all the other M&SWJR stations combined! The up platform, used for disembarking troops as well as passengers, was 835 ft in length when a typical passenger platform at the time was 300 ft long.

A Ludgershall train waits at Tidworth, 1948. (P J Garland Collection)

In the years up to the First World War, the station steadily expanded. The GWR took over much of its operation, as the resources of the M&SWJR were stretched to their limit. Incoming supplies such as coal, meat, flour and, of course, ordnance were all brought in by train. But it was not all one-way traffic since the garrison exported, among other things, dog droppings for the tanneries in the Midlands and horse manure for the strawberry and flower beds of Hampshire. The Tidworth Branch itself was closed in July 1963.

The Tidworth Garrison Military Railway

While Tidworth station was a military destination as well as a passenger one, it was in essence and practicality a transfer station for the internal railway that served the main barracks, garrison and hospital built for the army. Looking at a map of the garrison, it seems that a concerted effort was made to keep this part of the railway more in Wiltshire than in Hampshire.

Instead of the army's 'internal' railway running straight on from Tidworth station, it was reached by first reversing out of the station from the two lines that ran into it. These two lines soon ran 'backwards' into three, which ended at a considerable head shunt (a short piece of dead end track for shunting manoeuvres), before trains were propelled forward once more and into the garrison proper.

First there was a siding to the left that ran into an engine shed from which another line reversed across the main internal line and into a huge depot. The main internal railway, a single line branching right, skirted the Wiltshire/Hampshire border before finally crossing it by curving around to the left and arriving at the main barracks. Many of these were named after Indian army depots: the line passed Lucknow Infantry and Mooltan Cavalry Barracks on the right (a siding would reverse back across the border to serve these two properly), then doubled and served Jellalabad Infantry Barracks followed by Delhi Military Hospital and Candahar Infantry Barracks, shortly after which it curved to the right to serve Bhurtpore Infantry and Assaye Cavalry Barracks before finally coming to an end at Aliwal Cavalry Barracks. Along its route this served riding schools, rifle ranges, laundrettes, drill halls, bakeries and all kinds of other military buildings.

The line ran for 2½ miles and did not close until 1953. Traffic was considerable during the two world wars and between 1942 and 1946 a substantial American garrison was stationed here.

What Is Left Today

With the closure of the M&SWJR/GWR in 1961, the route between Grafton Junction and Ludgershall has been reclaimed by nature, though it can still be seen in places on embankments and earthworks. The military traffic was the salvation of this section of the M&SWJR though its very rural nature was its undoing in the end.

However, while the internal military railway is now history, the Tidworth branch from Ludgershall has actually survived better than one might expect. In fact, there has been an extension to some parts of this railway, though with the M&SWJR gone, it has to be reached from Andover.

The platforms at Ludgershall have mostly disappeared under housing estates but a few traces can be seen. The goods yard still exists for military traffic and the Tidworth Branch still curves away to the left just before reaching it. It runs past the same sidings as it once did but these have grown in size and a small loco shed for the branch diesel shunter has been added. It continues on past a medical equipment depot on the right, with associated sidings, which is relatively recent. The line then runs parallel to a head shunt from the medical depot before curving round to the left and to a passing loop. From here it curves left again to a vehicle depot and sidings which were laid down in 1943.

4
The Midland & South Western Junction Railway: 3

Marlborough Low Level to Savernake High Level

The story of the short but critical stretch of line between Marlborough Low Level and Savernake High Level is not just that of the M&SWJR but also one of a railway man and his effect on that railway.

By 1891, the M&SWJR was in a parlous state. Rundown rolling stock, stations in disrepair and track being taken over by nature were the problems that could be seen by passengers using the line. However, to the accountants and the Board the situation appeared even worse. Between 1881 and 1882 the company had gone through a succession of senior managers, including one traffic manager, two general managers and two secretaries, all of whom had been unable to improve or even to arrest the downward spiral of the company and it had gone into receivership in 1884. But cometh the hour, cometh the man and towards the end of 1891 the directors of the M&SWJR sought advice from the manager of the L&SWR on securing the services of a new general manager, the L&SWR's Sam Fey.

Sam Fey Steps In!

Sam Fey had joined the London and South Western Railway Company in 1872 and by 1891 had reached the position of assistant storekeeper. Known for being hard-working and skilful, he seemed an ideal candidate for this new post and was appointed General Manager and Secretary of the M&SWJR in February 1892. All of the senior officers were dismissed except Mr J.R. Shopland, who was kept on as Engineer. The then-current receiver, Lt Colonel F.D. Grey, who had been in the post since 1884 and, by all accounts, never saw eye to eye with the Board, was persuaded to leave office and Fey then took this position as well.

Now he had complete control of the M&SWJR, a situation that these days would no doubt raise many an eyebrow. But in 1893, it was the beginning of a new chapter in the history of the M&SWJR. When Fey took over it was said he had to wait for the station takings to come in before the staff could be paid. But, after five years, receipts had risen by more than 60% and, after reaching agreement with its creditors, the M&SWJR was freed from receivership in November 1897.

The Marlborough and Grafton Railway

Yet problems still remained. Nothing would ever be right until the company could free itself from the restrictions imposed upon it by working over the GWR lines, especially the critical stretch between Marlborough Junction and Wolfall Junction, just past Savernake. As already stated, the GWR charged the M&SWJR a hefty toll for using this stretch of line but its hostile business practices did not help either. In one remarkable instance a Great Western ticket inspector tried to charge a M&SWJR manager a fare for travelling on the footplate of one of his own engines! The steep gradient of this stretch was a further problem, with fully loaded trains struggling to cover it. Attempts to make improvements just met with unsurprising intransigence on the part of the GWR.

So, in 1894, it was decided to build a new line between Marlborough, Savernake and Wolfall/Grafton junctions. The biggest obstacle to the project was Savernake Forest, owned by the Marquess of Ailesbury. However, since the Marquess was a shareholder in the M&SWJR, it could be argued that it was in his interest to back this ambitious plan. The new line was intended to be only 5¾ miles long, under a separate company (since the M&SWJR was still in receivership) to be called the Marlborough and Grafton Railway. The Marquess was quite willing to help this new company but laid down two conditions to the promoters. First, he would charge rent of £450 a year for the use of the land and second, he wanted his own private waiting room at the new Savernake High Level station when it was built. He also stipulated that these facilities should be close to, and as good as, the ones at GWR's Savernake (Low Level) station and that certain trains should stop at the new station for his use. With the backing of the War Department, which was building the nearby Tidworth Barracks, and despite the unsurprising fierce opposition of the GWR, the bill for the new line was passed in August 1896.

The line was to take a more direct route to Savernake, continuing on instead of crossing over to the GWR line from Marlborough South Junction, and thus avoiding any turns or curves. This would also lessen the impact of construction on the Marquess's land, as the new line could be squeezed in between the GWR line and the edges of Savernake Forest. From an engineering point of view, the main undertaking was to build the double-track, 648-yard-long Marlborough tunnel. This ran in a deep cutting with almost sheer chalk walls 70 ft high on either side of the entrances. However, these walls were prone to collapse after bad weather, especially in the winter, requiring the tunnel to be cleared out. Georgiana, Marchioness of Ailesbury, laid a keystone above the southern entrance on 2nd July 1898 (though the line opened on 26th June). Then, on 1st August 1899, the Marlborough and Grafton Railway became absorbed into the M&SWJR.

From 1943 to 1950, a military siding ran into an Ordnance Depot in Savernake Forest, two miles south of Marlborough tunnel. Although its existence was short, it did see a horrific accident in January 1946 when an explosion occurred, killing eight soldiers and injuring many more. Some 29 wagons and three lorries were also destroyed. However, the bravery of Captain Biggs and Sergeant Robertson, who worked through the flames to move burning wagons and help others, prevented more than 2,000 tons of other ordnance exploding and saved another 69 wagons. For their efforts they each were awarded a George Cross.

The Running of the Line

With a complex track plan between Marlborough, Savernake and Grafton Junction, operating on these lines was never consistent or straightforward. This was sometimes due to maintenance but it was also because of the conditions laid down by the Marquess of Ailesbury. For

Granville Manor *hauling a Cheltenham train at Savernake High Level,*
1948. (P J Garland Collection)

instance, Savernake Low and High Level stations were
used for the same service but at different times.

To begin with, Marlborough South Junction was taken
out of service in 1898. This severed the new line from the
GWR branch line. (This junction was reinstated in 1926,
three years after the M&SWJR had been swallowed up by
the GWR, so that the old GWR station at Marlborough
could be used as a goods terminal.) The new line was a
double one but from May 1933, when the GWR station at
Marlborough (High Level) closed for passengers, both lines
became bi-directional. Branch line trains would use the
western line and M&SWJR trains would use the eastern
line. A junction at Hat Gate, not far out of Savernake
station, allowed branch line trains to leave Savernake Low
Level but still use the 'new line' to Marlborough. A

chronology of the line says that this was when the line was 'singled': possibly the case from the M&SWJR perspective.

However, in a track plan from 1954, things had changed yet again! Due to a chalk fall on the 'High Level Line' all trains began to use Savernake Low Level. By this time the line was being wound down and the GWR had been absorbed into BR Western Region. The track plan around Grafton Junction and Savernake was rationalised, with some stretches of the 'spare' line being taken up. To illustrate the parlous nature of the route by then, the last passenger train taking boys to Marlborough College hauled by a Western Region Hymek Diesel Hydraulic came to grief when it ran off the track where it had recently been lifted! The line and route closed very soon afterwards.

5
The Midland &
South Western Junction
Railway: 4

From Swindon Town to Cricklade
via Rushey Platt

Financially and historically, the future of the M&SWJR depended upon extending the M&SWJR north from Swindon. But it was not until July 1881 when the Swindon & Cheltenham Extension Railway (S&CER for short), was incorporated that the plan was put into action.

The building of this stretch was to follow a familiar pattern. First the S&CER locked horns with the GWR, which prepared a plan to show the unsuitability of the S&CER's route by highlighting the gradients involved. The engineer of the S&CER, James R. Shopland, countered these accusations by pointing out that the GWR's plans were inaccurate, showing Southampton as more than 200 ft higher than it actually is!

By April 1882, work on the new line had started and was well advanced when the GWR began legal action to stop this fledgling company from building the line on land around Swindon. The action failed but the S&CER had no financial plan for the building of the line. It was left to the contractors, Watson, Smith and Watson to offer to carry out the work and this was accepted. It was pointed out, though, that creating a company of such limited scope (serving only Swindon to Cheltenham, on paper at least) would adversely affect investment into the company.

Around this time the local railway companies changed their approach to tackling the hostility of the GWR and tried to come to some agreement with the L&SWR, which had been waging its own war against the GWR for some time. In 1883, various sections of the M&SWJR asked it to run their lines for them, but the L&SWR entered into an agreement with the GWR instead, coming to peaceful terms with them in an attempt to keep other railways and therefore competition out of each other's territory.

So, it could be considered an amazing feat that towards the end of 1883 the first stretch of the line from Rushey Platt to Cirencester was opened at all, though not without problems. September–December rainfall in 1883 was said to have been heavier than for that period in any of the previous 50 years and this caused landslides, which took days to clear. While the infrastructure of the line was built for double track, single track was laid throughout. The line was passed for passenger use on 17th December 1883.

The S&CER was operated by the SM&AR under an agreement of June 1882 but to all intents and purposes, it was initially a part of the SM&AR. The two amalgamated on 23rd June 1884 to formally become the Midland and South Western Junction Railway. But by now, the game was all but up.

The contractors, Watson, Smith and Watson went bankrupt in 1885 and had been freed from their contract at the end of the previous year. At the same time a receiver was appointed to the M&SWJR after a petition from the company's own engineer who had a debt against the company of more than £5,500. The only way out was to carry on with the extension of the line towards Cheltenham to justify the building of the railway in the first place and shareholders were persuaded to wait for the completion of the northern extension.

The story does have a happy ending. The extension was completed; with the appointment of Sam Fey to take control of the company, and the opening of the 'new Marlborough line', the future of the Midland and South Western Junction Railway was assured for the time being.

The Route Explained

The distance between the station at Swindon Town and Rushey Platt was only about 1½ miles. For three months, Rushey Platt was the terminus of the SM&AR until the GWR undertook to link it up with their own station via a curve at Swindon Junction. This curve met their main line a little further on and was used mostly for freight. Passengers were carried until 1885 but the GWR had followed their usual practice of extorting a high price to use the curve and the track to their Swindon station and when the SM&AR used it for passenger services between 1882 and 1885, the service lost £1,500 per year! Interestingly, the curve was mixed gauge until 1892 so GWR broad gauge trains could use it as well.

Rushey Platt was quite a big station and by 1885 it boasted a subway and four platforms. At first two served the curve to Swindon Junction where the main station building was located. But when the S&CER was extended towards Cheltenham on a bridge over the GWR main line, another couple of very short platforms were built here, staggered and on a different level to the old main ones. Though the level of passengers was never very high, there was considerable freight of coal, milk and timber, some of which used a small goods yard here. By 1905 the station needed refurbishment and with too few passengers to justify the work, it closed except to freight, though (unofficially it seems) passengers still used it for some years after.

The bridge over the GWR main line was built for double track but only carried a single line until it was altered to carry a siding which doubled as a passing loop. Beyond this we come to Moredon Halt, a 40 ft platform at the base of a bridge used for loading milk churns. Though passengers occasionally used the Halt, it was never mentioned in timetables. Opposite this were sidings into a coal-fired power station. This considerable collection of buildings with its cooling tower and chimney dominated the surrounding countryside until its demolition in 1979, some six years after its actual closure.

Another long passing loop here gave the impression that the line to Blunsdon, the next station, was double-track. Opened in 1895, this station was also used mainly for milk traffic. The little station buildings were made of corrugated iron on a wooden platform and the siding curved away from the line so sharply that locomotives were banned from using it. Only trains drawing enough wagons to be able to pick up any waiting wagons in the siding were allowed to use the station. After the First World War there was a daily passenger service to Blunsdon but this ceased in 1928 and the station closed completely in the mid-1930s.

The next station, Cricklade, the last inside Wiltshire, opened a day after the official passing of the line for passenger service. But it was an important event for this town, which could only be reached by roads of dubious quality. Double-track through the station, the platforms were built quite large in anticipation of the expected traffic.

Four sidings were built, serving a goods yard that included cattle pens and a goods shed. By the end of the First World War, milk traffic was such that the loading stage for it had been rebuilt twice and so heavy was the demand that Cricklade continued for freight some two years after it was closed to passengers.

Rebirth, Revival and Remains

Despite the eventual closure of the M&SWJR, at Blunsdon one small section of the line has seen a dramatic revival. Formed in 1978, the Swindon and Cricklade Railway (SCR) has run on the former trackbed from Blunsdon to a new

Shortly before reaching the old Swindon Town station, the M&SWJR track bed goes through this short tunnel. (Author)

Remains of the up platform on the upper Rushey Platt station on the M&SWJR track bed. (Author)

station at Hayes Knoll, three quarters of a mile away, since 1998. Though Blunsdon is short and basic, with storage sidings around a rebuilt station and signal box, the SCR has quite a collection of shunting locomotives, both steam and diesel, along with assorted coaching stock. With support from the local authorities it is hoped to extend this fledgling railway south towards Swindon and north towards Cirencester. Perhaps, the M&SWJR might make a comeback yet, in a small way!

Aside from this revival a good deal of the track bed of the M&SWJR can still be walked. One such stretch is the 1½-mile section from Swindon Town to Rushey Platt. This is now a bridlepath, walkway and cycleway and is a nice diversion, taking in some great views of the hills and valleys south of Swindon. As a rather odd beginning to the walk you first have to make your way through an industrial park before you come across a footpath hidden in the corner that leads to the old track bed. This park is on the site of Swindon Town station and the old M&SWJR office building still stands over it. Walking under Devizes Road Bridge the route continues in a gentle curve, first in a deep cutting known for its geological features before opening on to an embankment to Rushey Platt via a bridge over the canal a long way below. Keen observers might be able to spot the remains of the upper level platforms and signal box at Rushey Platt. The lower level track bed and station are now under a car dealership next to the A3102.

6
Swindon (GWR) to Highworth

Swindon in the early 1960s, facing Paddington. (Lens of Sutton)

The story of the Swindon and Highworth Railway (S&HR) in some ways mirrors that of the M&SWJR: ambitious plans and lack of finances saw the route in trouble from the beginning. Even though the hope was to build the line to Lechlade it only reached Highworth, and eventually it found itself in the hands of the GWR. Between

Swindon and Highworth the line would serve just three stations: Stratton, Stanton and Hannington. Until recently, however, a short stretch of the line was still being used.

The Beginning

Royal Assent for building the S&HR was granted on 21st June 1875, which was declared a public holiday in Highworth, but the joy was short-lived. By 1877 less than a third of the £21,000 budget had been raised. The directors tried to tempt subscribers by offering half a crown to anyone raising £10 and by 1878 subscriptions were around £11,000; it was another year before a contractor was found to build the line and only then by being offered 850 shares in the company as part-payment!

Work began on 6th March 1879 but an accident marred the opening ceremony. As the *North Wilts Herald* reported, the area cordoned off for the dignitaries, directors, shareholders and ladies became so full that the stand gave way and they all landed on top of each other!

In 1880 a further £8,000 had to be found to relay the track. The S&HR was being built as a light railway but, as the GWR had agreed to operate it, the line had to meet their standards. Further delay followed the inspection by Colonel Yolland of the Board of Trade in March 1881, which refused to approve it for passenger operation. Problems with the permanent way, a lack of lighting at level crossings and lax controls on the signalling were just a few of the concerns. This led to a vote of no-confidence in the engineer of the railway, the aptly-named Arthur Pain, who was sacked but refused to go quietly and pursued a bitter dispute with the company for some time. With no money left, in August 1882 the S&HR sold itself to the GWR for £16,000, giving shareholders a return of approximately 24%.

The necessary improvements were carried out and the line was passed fit for passenger operation in April 1883. The opening ceremony took place on 8th May when a train of ten coaches and four brake vans hauled by two engines left Highworth, taking half an hour to reach Swindon and returning to Highworth an hour later.

It became clear to the GWR that restrictions were needed to ensure safe running. As the line didn't meet the GWR standard for loading gauge, only tank engines could be used, along with the smaller four-wheeled coaches. This avoided another requirement of the last inspection, a turntable at Highworth, since a tank engine without a tender could run either way without having to be turned. The steep gradient (1 in 44) meant using a brake van with freight trains at all times, staffed with two or more guards. To begin with, five trains a day ran each way. However, the little branch line acquired some rather sizeable additions.

The Route

The S&HR route began at the Swindon GWR station, known then as Swindon Junction. The station was opened in 1842, with buildings designed by Isambard Kingdom Brunel. It was built, however, by the contractors, J & C Rigby, to which company the GWR granted a lease on the station's refreshment rooms. It was further agreed that all trains would stop here for at least ten minutes for refreshments. With railway mania came an appetite for speed and this ten-minute stop became a headache to the GWR, which also got complaints for the service and

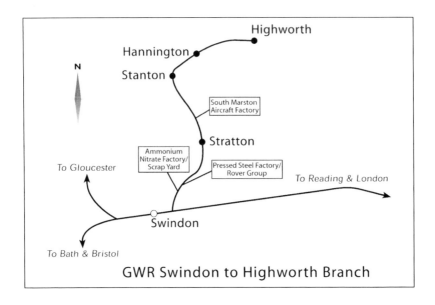

GWR Swindon to Highworth Branch

quality of the food and drink, including one from Brunel himself. Eventually the GWR bought the lease back in 1895 for £100,000!

The station was originally built with two large island platforms and a multitude of tracks beside and between them. Bay platforms were later added and a subway linking them all. By 1933 sidings dominated either end of the station. Over time, the station, along with the Swindon railway works (see Chapter 1), has changed dramatically. The track has been reduced by some 80%, and the right island platform and buildings have gone. A new platform was built for postal traffic on the main line, but this looks very modern and out of character with Brunel's building. The entrance today is disappointing for such an important station and is now located at the base of the Signal Point tower block that stands over the station with its huge BR

The modern day Swindon station with Brunel's building on what is now
platforms 1, 2 & 3, overshadowed by Signal Point Tower behind the new
platform 4 on the right. (Author)

logo at the top. The left island platform remains with two
through platforms and a bay platform for local services.

Highworth Line services left from here at the opposite
end at what was platform seven. The route ran east up the
GWR main line, leaving it at Highworth Junction, just past
Swindon goods yard. A vast factory works on the left,
which produced ammonium nitrate for munitions use in
the First World War and was used by Plessey & Co as a
supply depot during the Second World War, had its own
internal railway serving many sidings and an engine house
for the five tank engines that worked here. A couple of

81

sidings remain, running from the original points to serve European Metal Recycling (EMR). In 1958 a company was set up across the line to make car bodies. This passed into the hands of the Rover Cars Group and had its own internal railway worked by six Fowler diesel locomotives. By 1965 the Highworth line ended not far beyond amid a set of four sidings for shunting from the various metal firms.

Until 1965 the line continued via a gentle curve to the north-east and the first station it came to was Stratton. Just 1¼ miles from Highworth Junction and clustered around and under a bridge, Stratton had a passing loop and a couple of sidings serving milk traffic and later the nearby Trinidad Asphalt plant and Arkells Brewery, delivering hops, malt, sugar and coal.

Before the next station at Stanton another little detour at South Marston was a short branch line that during the Second World War served a Vickers Armstrong aircraft factory building Spitfires, among other things. This branch ran into a cutting, before it reached a little halt for the factory workers and two passing loops. There was no public service here. The line ran under a bridge carrying the A361 into the factory itself. The works were used again in the Suez Crisis (1956–57) and the branch line continued to serve a factory until the Highworth line closed in 1965. The cutting was later filled in.

Further up the Highworth line we reach Stanton, located not far from the disused Stanton Mill. This was the original Vickers factory. A single platform to the right of the line boasted a station house, the only station other than the terminus at Highworth to have one. Ironically, by the time it had been built, the post of stationmaster had been abolished because traffic was too low. In 1923 there were three staff at Stanton but by 1929 only one porter. Behind

Highworth station looking back towards Hannington, 1952. (Joe Moss Collection)

the station were a couple of sidings that were used for local agricultural goods though milk traffic here was lighter than at the other stations. During the First World War a temporary siding was laid just south of the station to load timber from the nearby woods. By 1949 Stanton was reclassified as a halt and became unstaffed. It closed completely by 1953 though the line was still used for freight.

The next station, Hannington, was not much larger than Stanton, with a passing loop and one siding. The village could boast only 201 inhabitants by the turn of the 20th century and milk was the main traffic, which at its peak was delivering up to 100 churns a day to a special milk train that ran on the Highworth line.

End of the line at Highworth station, 1952. (Joe Moss Collection)

Hannington was the lowest point on the line and the high point was the terminus at Highworth, reached by a steep gradient.

Built on a curve, the line split into two for a passing loop in front of the single platform. A reversible siding had a goods shed at one end. At the end of the platform a cattle pen and milk dock were situated to serve the market, which closed at the end of the 1920s. An interesting export from Highworth was oriental carpets from the nearby Vorda works.

The Decline and the End

The Highworth line stopped carrying passengers in March 1953. It remained opened for goods until August 1962 and

84

The Rover car plant is on the right and the Highworth branch continues on the far left. Disused container wagons now lie stored on the sidings. (Author)

though commuter trains to Swindon ran during this period, these were never advertised to the general public. Milk was a major source of traffic on the route but when this switched to road transport it was the beginning of the end for the line.

The only stretch left is a short piece of line just before Stratton between the Rover factory and the European Metal Recycling plant. Today a footpath and cycle way run parallel to the line from the main road, the B4143, through to Stratton. There is still the stub of a siding into EMR's plant and they tell me that traffic is still sent by rail to their depots in Liverpool and South Wales about twice a week.

85

However, the sidings into the car plant have not been used since the closure of the Rover factory at Longbridge and are now used to store container wagons. The points and track into the factory are now gated and padlocked on both sides of the footpath. Further up, the footpath crosses the single-track line by a little timber level crossing amid a small wood on the edge of Swindon. This is gated and fenced off. Beyond this more container wagons now sit rusting away on sidings rapidly being overgrown. This is where the line truly ends. Past Stratton the route is still traceable along the track bed. At Highworth all has been lost except for the tell-tale Station Road, the old station approach, now leading into a little cluster of houses called 'Fairview'.

7
A Military Railway

*From the L&SWR Main Line at Grateley
to Bulford Camp*

The Bulford Branch Line begins in Hampshire but the majority is in Wiltshire, and like parts of the Ludgershall Branch, it owes its existence to Salisbury Plain. As well as being home to Stonehenge and other associated burial mounds and earthworks, for over a hundred years the area has been used for training by the Army and the RAF. It is not surprising, therefore, that a vast logistical network was set up to support this, including four railways and no less than five aerodromes.

The GWR and L&SWR fight for Salisbury Plain

At first all the railways in this area skirted the Plain, but it was not long before the GWR and the L&SWR turned their attention to it and joined battle. The first round began in 1882 when the L&SWR proposed a route from their Basingstoke–Salisbury main line at Grateley across Salisbury Plain to Amesbury, and on to Shrewton and Westbury before finally reaching Bristol. The last stretch to Bristol would be via either the Somerset and Dorset Railway or the North Somerset Railway. The route would be known as the Bristol and London & South Western Railway.

A Bill was put before Parliament in November 1882. The route was a blatant attempt by the L&SWR to steal traffic from the GWR's Bristol–London line and, interestingly, it originally ran so close to Stonehenge that Sir John Lubbock, the chief spokesman for archaeology in Parliament, demanded that it be diverted. The bill was defeated in 1883. Not content with their victory the GWR then tried their hand at a railway route across Salisbury Plain.

The GWR's route would run from Pewsey, which was already on their main line between Devizes and Newbury, and run southwards across the Plain via their station at Salisbury. It would then cut across L&SWR territory to Southampton. Not surprisingly, the L&SWR fought this scheme and, while in July 1883 an act was granted for part of the route (known as the Pewsey and Salisbury Railway), the Salisbury to Southampton section was defeated. Perhaps the GWR decided to cut their losses or, more likely, decided that without the final section the project was not worthwhile, but in any event the line was never built.

The Light Railways Act of 1896

Today the term 'light railway' brings to mind expensive inner light transit schemes such as the Docklands Light Railway in London and Manchester's Metro Tramway. In 1896 it meant something very different.

The Light Railways Act of 1896 granted permission for railways to be built 'on the cheap', using as little material, labour, money and parliamentary approval as possible, in less populated and remote areas of the countryside. This prompted the GWR to present a revised route which left Salisbury at Bemerton, and travelled on to Pewsey up the Avon valley via Amesbury. The station at Amesbury would be sited so near to Stonehenge that a tentative station name was 'Stonehenge and Amesbury'. In August 1898, the GWR Pewsey and Salisbury Light Railway Order was granted.

The Military Steps In!

Around this time the War Department began to buy up Salisbury Plain and entered into negotiations with the L&SWR for their own light railway to serve the military camps proposed for the area. The idea was for a light railway to run from Grateley on the main line via Newton Tony and Amesbury to Shrewton, more or less in the middle of the Plain. With such a direct route the line might serve the community as well as the military. Authorisation was granted for the 'Amesbury & Military Camp Light Railway' in September 1898.

At this point the GWR route hit the buffers, so to speak. Their Light Railway Order stipulated that if their route crossed War Department land (now a good deal of Salisbury Plain!) they had to have Army consent. It is perhaps a good thing that no public railway going anywhere near Stonehenge came to anything in the end. Stonehenge was afforded much less protection then. While the Army used it in manoeuvres, it was reported in the *Guardian* newspaper that the sound of chiselling and hammering could be heard all day long as tourists sought either to leave their mark upon the stones or to take a piece home with them!

A third railway company now appeared on the scene. The M&SWJR planned an extension from their line at Ludgershall station on the eastern side of the plain to run to Bulford and then on to Amesbury, approaching the same destinations as the GWR and L&SWR from the opposite direction. Although the route was never built, an extension was built as far as Tidworth (see chapter 3).

89

Building the Line

The L&SWR and the War Department wasted no time in getting construction of their light railway under way. In January 1899 a contract worth £62,517 was awarded to J. F. Firbank. Firbank was no stranger to railway construction in the South West and had already taken part in constructing the Basingstoke to Alton Light Railway. Locomotives of the 0-6-0 variety were used: compact but heavy-duty workhorses.

In November 1899, however, with construction advancing, the Army changed their mind! Instead of going on to Shrewton in the middle of the plain they decided to loop back from Amesbury to the large camp being built at Bulford. This cut the length of the line from ten to four miles, leaving Firbank and the L&SWR in consternation, with work already begun beyond Amesbury. The L&SWR obtained an abandonment order for this section and Firbank was compensated with the promise of other work elsewhere on their network.

Leaving the main line after Grateley there would eventually be a total of five stations on the 'new' route: Newton Tony, Amesbury, Bulford, Bulford Camp and lastly, Sling. The first section to Amesbury was completed for goods traffic by April 1902 and for passengers by June. However, in March it was reported in the *Salisbury and Winchester Journal* that troops embarked on the 21st at Amesbury for the start of their long journey to the war in South Africa. Ironically, when the first official passenger train arrived in Amesbury on 2nd June, it brought the early morning newspapers with the front page news that the war was over!

The extension to Bulford Camp and Sling was granted a Light Railway Order in January 1903 and was to be called the 'Amesbury & Military Camp Light Railway (Bulford Extension)' thereby giving the line its name. Work began in 1904 and the line was built by the L&SWR under their chief engineer J.W. Hood and his assistant Mr Short. Passenger services began running to Bulford in June 1906.

A Look at the Bulford Branch Line

Though the Bulford Branch Line began at Grateley in Hampshire on the Basingstoke to Salisbury main line, it cannot be ignored in the context of the line. Grateley station was expanded with the up platform turned into an island platform, and a terminus for Bulford line trains added. Extra sidings were built to accommodate the extra, mainly military traffic. The Bulford Branch line then ran 'up' parallel to the Basingstoke–Salisbury line so for a short distance there were three running lines. At Amesbury

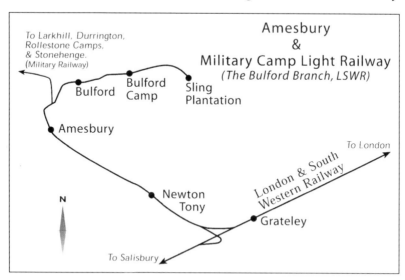

Junction the track branched left to Newton Tony and Amesbury, then on to Bulford, Bulford Camp and Sling at the end of the line.

In 1901 the branch line was just a single track branching from the L&SWR main line. However, traffic on this branch grew so fast and to make the journey from Salisbury to Bulford a lot easier in 1904 a double track from what became known as Newton Tony Junction was added to build the Newton Tony Curve linking it to the L&SWR main line. However, so the down Bulford line would not need to cross the up main line it was decided to tunnel under both main lines and have the down Bulford line join the down main line a little way beyond the junction. Back at Newton Tony Junction, the Bulford line was double track all the way to Amesbury.

Newton Tony was the first station on the line. Rather conventional with the two lines running between platforms, it had four sidings for goods and cattle. Next came Amesbury, the original terminus of the line. Emerging from a chalk cutting, passengers from Newton Tony would suddenly find themselves pulling into a vast station with two large island platforms, a third island 'docking' platform, four sidings and four lines running between them. At the Newton Tony end lay two more sidings and at the Bulford end, four long 'Shrewton' sidings for berthing troop trains. At the height of the First and Second World Wars, this station would, at times, have been extremely busy, with the movement of hundreds, if not thousands, of troops and supplies. Amesbury was the headquarters of the NAAFI and this alone created a fair amount of traffic.

Next came Bulford station, serving the village itself, the line here having turned sharply away from Amesbury and passing Ratfyn Junction which led to the Larkhill Military

*A damaged yet useful photograph of a train at Bulford station in 1930.
(H F Wheeller Collection)*

Railway. Having been single track since Amesbury, Bulford
station still had a passing loop. Beyond this lay the single
line to Bulford Camp where a long siding served a wide,
desolate platform. Three-quarters of a mile further on came
the end of the line at Sling, where there was one island
platform serving a siding and a passing loop. Though Sling
station fell into disuse between the wars, during the Second
World War the War Department asked the Southern
Railway to reopen it and to relay the track.

Decline, Closure and What's Left of the Line

Perhaps the most ironic thing about the Amesbury &

A train stands at Amesbury station on the Bulford Branch in 1955. (R S Carpenter)

Military Camp Light Railway was that it was anything but. Double-track for half its length, with cuttings and embankments and stations like Amesbury on its route, it was more like a proper country branch line, but one that increasingly depended on military traffic.

With most of the railway's commercial passenger traffic coming from Salisbury, it began to feel the pinch when better bus services started to run in the area in the late 1940s. Fuel cuts then all but suspended the passenger service and when it began again, there was just one train each weekday! Eventually the public service was withdrawn completely and the last train ran on 28th June 1952. Though Amesbury and Bulford stations remained open for goods and military traffic, Newton Tony closed for good. In October 1954, the line was 'singled' and

94

The track bed of the old Bulford Branch runs parallel with the current Waterloo–Salisbury main line, seen from the present Grateley station. (Author)

realigned and the Salisbury Curve was shut. Two daily goods trains still ran through and military trains continued to run as and when required. Transport for the NAAFI also generated some traffic, as did 'enthusiasts' specials', but on 4th March 1963, the line closed for good and the track was lifted in 1965.

Grateley station is a shadow of its former self. In fact, as if to emphasise this fact it won the 'Best Unstaffed Station' Award in 1994, a dubious distinction! The island platform that served the line to Bulford is fenced on one side and serves the main line through the station, though only slow trains now stop here. The track bed behind the fence is used

An old railway signal stands at the base of the embankment for the old Bulford station and station approach road. (Author)

to store sections of concrete cable ducting. The old track bed is still clearly visible beside the main line towards Salisbury.

At Newton Tony and Amesbury all trace of the railway has disappeared. Bulford Camp is still used and can be viewed from various points around the A303 and the B3028; and the track bed on the edge of the camp is visible.

Leaving Bulford the road crosses over the Avon before going uphill. Here you pass a tall, wide, man-made grassy embankment on your left. Next to the base of this embankment, at the entrance to the old station approach road which is now residential, looking somewhat out of place but still standing tall, is a worn and battered railway signal! From the embankment you can see a small office complex and car park on the site of the old station, but looking over the road that the railway once crossed, to the green fields opposite, any trace of the route has disappeared completely.

The Larkhill Military Railway and Rails to Stonehenge!

With the run-up to the First World War, the military presence on Salisbury Plain increased considerably. More camps were set up and so it was planned to build another extension to the Bulford Branch. Opening in 1914 and branching away to the left at Ratfyn Junction between Amesbury and Bulford, this crossed the Avon before serving some sidings known as 'flying shed sidings' or the 'flying shed' branch, where the Bristol Flying School was located before it moved to Surrey in 1914.

The line now entered Larkhill Camp, then Durrington Camp, after which the line to Rollestone Camp, where there was a Balloon School, went straight on while another track branched to the left towards Fargo Hospital and some hangars owned by Handley Page, the aircraft company.

Beyond Rollestone the main line ran straight on to Lakedown airfield and Druids Lodge and another branch to the left served Stonehenge airfield, a stone's throw from Stonehenge itself. The Larkhill Military Railway was not run by the L&SWR but by the Southern Command of the Army's Camp Railways. It closed in 1929.

The Porton Camp Railway

Since the Second World War, Porton Down has become synonymous with the chemical and biological warfare experiments that are carried out there. But though what was Porton Camp and became Porton Down was not physically linked to the Bulford Branch like the Larkhill Military Railway, it is close enough to warrant a mention.

Porton Camp was originally built during the First World War as an experimental station for the Royal Engineers. Material and goods for the camp were transferred from the goods yard of Porton station – on the L&SWR main line, not far down the track from Newton Tony Junction – on to a narrow gauge railway which looped back around the goods yard before crossing the main line over an old farm bridge. A little way on it divided to go left and 'up' the line to Porton Camp, or right and 'down' to Winterbourne Gunner camp, which was used as a trench mortar experimental station.

As Porton Camp grew in size and importance, so did the railway. In the camp itself a maze of track served several factories. As the First World War drew to a close, passengers as well as cargo were being carried, with engines being steam-driven. A plan was drawn up to convert the narrow gauge into standard gauge but came to nothing after the war when traffic slumped. Buses took over much of the passenger service in the 1930s. Though the little railway increased in size again when the Chemical and Biological Warfare Centre opened in 1948 (using petrol-driven engines), road transport took over most supply work and the railway ceased in the late 1940s.

8

Two Gauges to Salisbury

The GWR and L&SWR in and around Salisbury and the Market House Branch

Salisbury has always been an important railway centre and was shared by the GWR and the L&SWR. When the L&SWR first arrived in 1847, a speaker at the opening ceremony's banquet announced that Salisbury should have the ambition of becoming 'the Manchester of the South'. With the main line from London Waterloo to the West passing through, Salisbury thankfully has become better known as 'the Gateway to the West'.

Leaving Salisbury by train today for Yeovil and the West Country, you would travel on the former L&SWR lines. You would need to look over to your right for an intermittent view of the old GWR route into and out of the city.

At one time the GWR and L&SWR ran on separate tracks, up and down, four in total, separated at times by an embankment and dense foliage. But as the GWR slowly disappeared from Salisbury, retreating under the expansion and growth of the L&SWR, rationalisation saw both companies sharing the latter's tracks. Though most of the GWR track was lifted in 1973, some of it is still used by English China Clays for its line to Westbury. The tracks finally divide at Wilton Junction: the L&SWR route to the left heads to Yeovil and Dorset via Gillingham (Wilton South) whilst the former GWR route to the right runs to Westbury and beyond (Wilton North).

In the days of steam however, Wilton South had a major part to play in the history of the famous express the *Devon Belle*. Although 'advertised' as a non-stop service from Waterloo to Sidmouth Junction, the L&SWR never had an engine with the water capacity to go the distance. So, to avoid pulling in at Salisbury, the engine was changed at Wilton South, a station too 'insignificant' to count as a stop!

The GWR at Salisbury

Brunel planned to introduce the Great Western broad gauge to Salisbury by way of the Wiltshire, Somerset & Weymouth Railway whose line to Warminster opened in 1851. After delays due to financial difficulties this was absorbed into the GWR and finally arrived on 30th June 1856 at a terminus at Fisherton Street, to the west of the city centre. This was not, however, the first railway into Salisbury. The L&SWR had arrived nine years previously from Bishopstoke (Eastleigh) on the London-Southampton main line, running in to a terminus at Milford to the south-west of the city.

The GWR terminus was a typical Brunel design, with two platforms either side of the tracks, down the middle under a part-glazed roof. This station remained broad gauge until the conversion to standard gauge in 1874. Close by and opening in 1858 was a broad gauge engine shed with two tracks which lasted until 1899 when a new three-track engine shed was built away to the west. By this time, the L&SWR Fisherton Street station next door (a footbridge linked the two) was expanding and having taken over the

The old GWR station with the left side of the station-turned-goods yard. The GWR water tower stands over the site, with a DMU train care depot behind. (Author)

site of the old engine shed, paid for the building of the new one. The original GWR terminus enjoyed remarkable longevity, however. With the L&SWR station next door being more in demand because it offered a through service, the GWR terminus closed to passengers in 1932 but continued to be used for freight until 1991!

Today, not all of this piece of Salisbury's railway history is lost. Firstly, the old large GWR water tank is still one of the most visible things in and around Salisbury station. Secondly, the main front building of the original station is now listed and is in commercial use. And lastly, making your way around the back of it, you will still find to this day, a portion of the left platform and canopy.

101

It is just enough to recall the days when the stretch of line between Salisbury and Wilton was a grand site for any railway enthusiast. From the days of steam (the West Country and Merchant Navy 4–6–2s on named trains such as the *Devon Belle* and the *Atlantic Coast Express*) to that class of locomotive unique to the Western Region in the 1960s and 1970s – the diesel hydraulics, including the Westerns, Warships and Hymeks – and then finally to the modern enthusiast's favourite, the Class 50s. All at one time raced out of the city on the up gradient, with the spire of the magnificent cathedral in the background.

The L&SWR at Salisbury

The story of the L&SWR, later Southern Region, at Salisbury is not so straightforward, especially in operational terms. Its railway first entered Salisbury at Milford to the south-east of the city and on 27th January 1847 the first train arrived. The opening ceremony was performed by the chairman of the L&SWR, W. J. Chapman who had also been voted MP for the city just two days before. Passenger services started on 1st March 1847.

A more direct L&SWR line to London arrived from Andover to the north-east in 1857. For a couple of years it had to reverse into the terminus at Milford. Then, in 1859, a new line, passing around the top of Salisbury through the 443-yards-long Fisherton tunnel (often referred to as Salisbury tunnel), linked up with a new L&SWR line from Gillingham called the Salisbury and Yeovil Railway to run into a new L&SWR station, also at Fisherton Street. This was built within a few feet of the GWR broad gauge terminus. The Milford terminus lost its passengers to Fisherton Street through station but continued to see

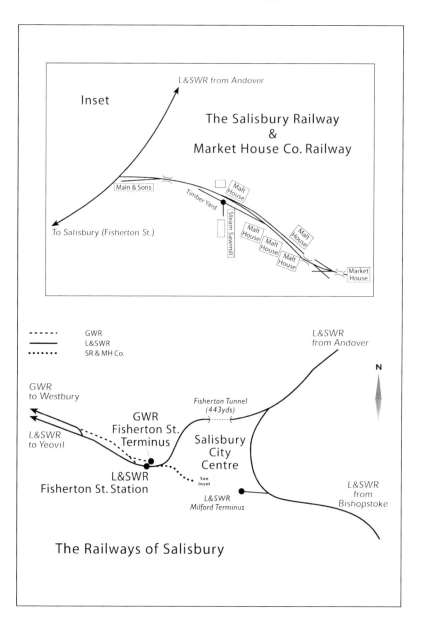

Inset

L&SWR from Andover

The Salisbury Railway
&
Market House Co. Railway

Main & Sons

Timber Yard

Malt House

Steam Sawmill

To Salisbury (Fisherton St.)

Malt House

Malt House

Malt House

Malt House

Malt House

Market House

------ GWR
——— L&SWR
••••••• SR & MH Co.

L&SWR
from Andover

N

GWR
to Westbury

Fisherton Tunnel
(443yds)

GWR
Fisherton St.
Terminus

Salisbury
City
Centre

L&SWR
to Yeovil

L&SWR
Fisherton St. Station

See
Inset

L&SWR
Milford Terminus

L&SWR
from
Bishopstoke

The Railways of Salisbury

103

heavy freight traffic to a goods depot converted from an engine shed on the site: a shunter was kept working almost 24 hours a day. The Milford terminus finally closed completely in 1967 and today the only visible sign that a railway was once there is a pub called the Railway Inn.

However, the L&SWR Fisherton Street station was not without problems. To begin with, it had only one platform serving both up and down trains, on the down side of the track! And to make things more confusing, a second 'ticket platform' was built past this station, also on the down side. So, while down trains in effect had two stops to make in Salisbury, up trains had first to run through the station to the ticket platform and then reverse back into the station proper – pity the poor passengers! The only concession to this operational nightmare was that the main platform was long enough to accommodate two trains at once, which meant they were back to back travelling in opposite directions!

In 1878 a new up platform was built, a short distance from the long down platform so up trains no longer had a need to reverse. Subways linked the up and down platforms. Then in 1902, the L&SWR finally got its act together and built the station we have today, i.e. four main platforms with through lines. The only survivor from the earlier station is the long down platform incorporated into the new ones.

Unfortunately, geography imposed other drawbacks. Being limited by Fisherton Street bridge at the east end, the station was entered from Fisherton tunnel on a sharp 8 chain curve. In 1906 this was the scene of a terrible accident when a boat train took the curve too quickly (more than twice the normal speed) and overturned, colliding with a milk train. Many of the 24 passengers killed were

The 'new' (1901/1902) and present L&SWR station with the 'old' (1859/1860) L&SWR station adjacent to it. Both have changed little since they were built. (Author)

Americans who had arrived at Plymouth on the S.S. *New York*. The injured Americans were cared for in Salisbury Infirmary and the then U.S. President, Theodore Roosevelt sent a 'Thank You' for taking care of them. It was after this accident that a speed restriction of 15 m.p.h. was imposed through Salisbury.

However, steam trains departing for London on this curve always faced a challenge to get away without too much wheel slip. One incident involved the railway photographer, George Heiron, who was having a cup of tea in a café close by to the station as a departing heavy steam-hauled train had so much trouble gaining traction that the vibration brought the ceiling in the café down!

At the west end of the station on the island platform a

two-storey brick building with tall chimneys and an outside staircase looks like a signal box. For a short while, it seems, it was used as such before the main Salisbury 'A' and 'B' signal boxes came into use. But since its closure, it has had a chequered life. It has been used to heat foot warmers for passengers, then as an office for carriage examiners, and is today used as a store for South-West Trains' refreshment trolleys!

The 'Market House Branch'

The Salisbury Railway and Market House Company Railway (SR&MH Co.) is often referred to as the 'Salisbury

The Market House Branch turned away sharply to the right where now the outside track curves to the left from the end of bay platform 6. (Author)

Market House Railway' or just simply the 'Market House Branch'. It had its origins in 1856 when Salisbury was all but ringed by railways. At only 460 yards/510 yards long (depending on what account you read and how you measure it), this branch line held the distinction of being the shortest independent standard gauge line in Britain. Curving away sharply to the right from what is now the end of bay platform 6, it was a freight-only branch formed by local businessmen concerned at the distance of the other stations from the city centre. At first it was horse-drawn but after a runaway train in 1868 the track was strengthened to take locomotives.

Three bridges carried it across three water courses and

The rear of the Market House has changed considerably since the new library was built within its walls. The bridge was the third and last one on the route. (Author)

the sidings along its route moved corn and seed for Main & Sons; supplies for Frederick Griffin & Co.'s steam sawmill; and coal and barley for Williams (Maltsters) Ltd. The Market House branch ran into the heart of the city to the market house proper, but its tracks inside the market building closed before the First World War. The line was gradually wound down and by the end of the Second World War its principal traffic was coal to the Salisbury Electric Light and Supply Co. The power station's change to fuel oil in 1962 meant the end for the branch, though it rather surprisingly lasted until 1964 under BR ownership.

The route of the branch today has mostly been built over. Where it left the main line is now a fitness gym, the car park of which includes the first bridge at its entrance. The last bridge into what was the market house still exists and is easily identifiable from old photographs. The large elegant market building remains but has changed over the years and is now a public library.

9
Military Camp Railways Around Salisbury

Although substantial, the army camps set up on and around Salisbury Plain often did not last long. They were built to demand, especially in the run-up to the First World War and to a lesser degree again in the Second World War. Many were sited as close to the Plain as possible and thus not far from Salisbury. To the west of the city two main railway lines were used as the starting point for three Military Camp branch lines. None was very big and like the camps they served, all trace of them is long since gone except for telltale earthworks.

The first was the Fovant Camp Branch line, leaving the L&SWR Salisbury–Exeter main line just after Dinton station. It was opened in October 1915, 2½ miles long and graded at 1 in 35. Leaving the south side of the down platform, trains for the camp crossed the river Nadder and ran through the village of Fovant before running around a hill above the village and then into the camp. While the railway and camp have long since gone one big reminder can be found on the side of Fovant Hill. Here, carved into the chalk is a series of large badges of regiments once stationed in the area. They can be seen from the A30 Salisbury–Shaftesbury Road where a plaque in a lay-by explains which badge is which.

Before the Second World War however the military was back. With an RAF depot nearby the many caves and limestone mines in and around Fovant and Chilmark were

109

used to store bombs. A two-foot gauge line was laid this time, some of it on the old railway. Exchange sidings were built to connect the narrow gauge lines with the standard gauge ones. These days the site is still owned by the Ministry of Defence and both sets of track are still there, though seldom used.

The Codford Camp Railway left the GWR Salisbury–Westbury line at Codford. This line, opening in October 1914, closed between 1922 and 1924 with the track being lifted in 1926. Leaving the line at Codford station, it almost doubled back on itself before curving north and crossing the Salisbury to Warminster Road, now the A36. After this it travelled through various barracks and camps before ending in the direction of Chitterne. A short branch left the camp railway southwards two-thirds of the way along to serve the camp hospital. After 1918 the GWR took over the running of the line before it closed.

The last military camp railway in the area was the Heytesbury Branch. Leaving Heytesbury, which was the next station after Codford, the 3½-mile-long branch was built to serve Sutton Veny Camp and the hospital there. It was designed so that hospital trains could draw up right alongside platforms serving the operating theatres built in 1916. The line was open from 1916 and closed between 1923 and 1926.

10
The Devizes Line

Holt Junction to Patney & Chirton
via Devizes

Devizes lies just to left of centre in Wiltshire between Salisbury Plain and the Marlborough Downs where three boundaries meet. It gets its name from the Roman term *ad divisas* meaning 'at the boundaries'. A big town with a market square, not unlike Salisbury, it is spread out in a rough semicircle around the base of a castle on a hill, a replica of which was rebuilt as a mansion in the 19th century. At its western edge is the Kennet and Avon Canal which climbs 230 feet through 29 locks at Caen Hill. In the 1800s this was the key form of transport to bring goods to the market.

Like Marlborough, it no longer has a railway although, in its railway heyday, Devizes had one of the largest stations in the county and between the wars this was worked by more than 30 staff. The line that ran through it was at times used as a main line. It saw famous trains such as the *Cornish Riviera Express* and the *Mayflower*, hauled by main-line locomotives using main-line coaching stock, and a few years before its closure it was visited by the *Flying Scotsman*.

After steam died out on the rail network, it was served by diesel rail cars and what were then, in the 1960s, the brand-new diesel hydraulics. It lasted just long enough to come under British Rail ownership. However, this was the age of the motor car and the Devizes line, now past its prime and lacking any major passenger destination, was seen as an extravagance and became one of Dr Beeching's biggest victims.

The Origins of the Line

The Devizes townspeople hoped that, when Brunel built his main line from London Paddington to Bath, it would run via their town; but instead it ran through Swindon. Likewise, when the GWR built their line from Newbury to Westbury it passed even closer but still failed to reach them.

By the mid-1850s Devizes was a booming market town – the traders and stall holders did not want to miss out and the canal now seemed slow. Some townspeople even invited Brunel to survey the area in the hope of a branch line. Though shares were allotted for this scheme, which became known as the 'Devizes and Melksham Great Western Branch Railway', it got no further. Then in 1845 an act was passed to build a line from Thingley Junction (on the GWR line from Swindon to Weymouth) via Melksham, Holt Junction and Westbury. Included in this were plans for expansion in Wiltshire including a branch to Devizes.

The act had originally been sponsored by the Wiltshire, Somerset and Weymouth Railway (WS&WR) and though plans were in place and land was being purchased for the Devizes branch, the company ran out of money and was propped up by the GWR. No sooner had the line from Thingley Junction to Westbury opened than it and the company were swallowed up by the GWR, which bought the WS&WR in 1850.

Even the Kennet and Avon Canal considered converting

their canal to a railway; then later planned a railway parallel with the canal (the Thames and Medway Canal in Kent ran a railway along one side and eventually the entire canal was converted). This new plan was titled the 'London, Newbury and Bath Direct Railway', but again it came to nothing.

Like Salisbury, Devizes found itself with railways on three sides (almost four if you count the short branch to Calne to the north-east, described in the next chapter) but not linked to them. In fact, the railway was only six miles from the town. Prominent townspeople, including the Mayor, Joseph Crockett, demanded a railway link. The GWR, not wanting them to go elsewhere, cooperated.

Brunel had proposed a plan for a GWR branch line from Thingley as early as 1844, but now an 8½-mile line to Devizes was built from the station at Holt Junction on the WS&WR. With stops at Semington Halt, Seend and Bromham & Rowde it completed the WS&WR's original 1845 plan. The construction was made more expensive by the steep gradient up Caen Hill, where the Kennet & Avon Canal has its famous flight of locks, but the GWR was kept from abandoning the project by lawsuits from the town. The track was broad gauge like most of the GWR routes at this time. The line opened on 1st July 1857, a week early. A public holiday was declared and all the shops were shut in Devizes, and at Holt a brass band played throughout the day. Passengers, it was reported in the *Devizes Gazette*, travelled between Holt and Devizes all day just for the fun of it, even though Holt Junction station was not open to the public at the same time as the opening of the line!

Devizes was a terminus for only five years. In November 1862 it became a major station on a through line with the expansion from Hungerford of the Berkshire and

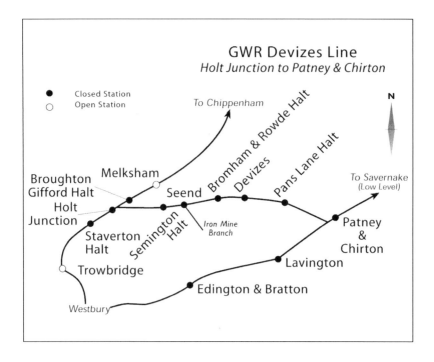

Hampshire Extension Railway. This route, again broad gauge, ran via Patney & Chirton, the delightfully named Pans Lane Halt and the tunnel under Devizes Castle. With Devizes now on a major north-east link between two GWR main lines it was able to advertise trains to London in both directions! And it was often used as a major route to London when the GWR main line was blocked, for example after a rock fall or landslide in or around Box Tunnel. The new through route saw expresses from Paddington to Weston-Super-Mare taking less than two hours to complete the 86-mile journey! This express would continue to run until the 1960s.

Description of the Line, Holt Junction to the Fish Bridge

Holt Junction at the beginning of the Devizes Line was situated on the WS&WR/GWR line between the Bradford Junctions and Melksham. The village of Holt is not far from Trowbridge, which at the beginning of the line's history was used as the starting point for passenger journeys. It was opened for use as an exchange station in 1861 and then finally to local traffic and passengers in April 1874. With a small island platform between the up and down lines, the only access to it was a footpath across the surrounding fields. It was not until 1877 that a road was provided along with a goods shed.

By the start of the 20th century the station had grown considerably: the platform had been widened (because the narrowness of the previous one was found to be dangerous when trains passed at speed), the tracks realigned, a footbridge provided to cross the tracks and platform lighting installed. By now the station had a large platform with waiting room (though for ladies only) and toilet facilities.

To cater for increased goods traffic it was equipped with four sidings serving a large goods shed and covered bay used for loading milk from the nearby Nestlé factory. Two sidings were built to serve this operation 1¾ miles further down the line at what became Staverton Halt but until they were run into the factory in 1934, the loading bay at Holt was still used. By 1913 the station buildings had been improved still further and two new sidings added. As time went by a station house, a parcels office and lamp room were built and two large timber name boards spelled out in big capitals 'Holt Junction for Devizes Branch'.

After Holt Junction the Devizes branch left the line going

115

eastwards and crossing the Avon over Whaddon Bridge. Originally a wooden structure built by Brunel, this was replaced in the 1880s by a more sturdy girder and caisson bridge. The line here was single-track and the next stop was Semington Halt, not far from Semington, a little village based around a workhouse, which was later converted into a hospital. The Kennet and Avon Canal also runs close by between the railway and the village. The station itself was a minor affair reached by a footpath up the railway embankment. It was not even standard height! By 1907 it had gained a little waiting shelter.

Little stations and halts like Semington were perfect for the unique GWR rail motors and auto trains. Rail motors were single coaches powered by an internal steam engine. Auto trains were made up of a small steam locomotive with two coaches, the last having a cab at the rear from which the train could be driven. Such trains could be called the precursors of the EMUs (Electric Multiple Units) and DMUs (Diesel Multiple Units) that populate the rail network today. Rail motors came with a set of fold-away steps so passengers would not have to climb down to platform level at halts like Semington. In 1909 its platform was replaced by a new, still minor one built of railway sleepers. RAF Melksham nearby was the destination for many of the passengers who used this little stop.

Leaving Semington, the line crossed a main road that ran parallel to the disused Wiltshire and Berkshire Canal before running on into Seend station.

Seend gets its name from being built on a sandy hill, the old English word for sand being 'send'. The station opened 14 months after the opening of the line and had only one platform to start with, with a road bridge at the Devizes end. In 1908 a down-side platform was added and the station became quite conventional with two tracks running between up and down platforms.

Trade was good to begin with, with passengers being able to buy Saturday–Monday return tickets to London. Trips to Weston-Super-Mare were also popular. Seend's heyday came around 1910 after which passenger traffic declined other than during the two world wars. By 1960 the station was unstaffed between 7 pm and 7 am the next day. By 1962, it was down to a single track and the last remaining porter was withdrawn.

However, Seend was close to some iron mines that also used the Kennet and Avon Canal nearby. These mines had been opened shortly before the opening of the line just a quarter of a mile away and there were long sidings at the station for shunting the ore wagons. The mines were large enough to warrant their own branch line that was at first double-track. After this, a collection of sidings and head shunts served the mines themselves. Unfortunately they were never very successful and changed hands several times. By 1886, the OS Map showed all of them as disused.

By 1924, this connection to the Devizes line had gone completely. Nonetheless, iron ore was still being extracted from a quarry on top of a nearby hill. To begin with it was transported to the sidings by horse and cart; then after the First World War an aerial ropeway was installed from the quarry to these sidings. In the 1920s the works burnt down and the aerial ropeway was dismantled in 1928. In the Second World War things picked up again but this was the last time.

The next station on the Devizes line was Bromham & Rowde Halt, opened in 1909. This was a single platform with a waiting shelter and a ticket office. Another little shelter was built for the freight traffic here: milk and

Bromham & Rowde Halt around 1960. (Lens of Sutton)

vegetables from the Bromham market gardens. A little goods loop was in use and by the 1920s a sawmill was operating close by. Because of this an extra siding at the station was added for transporting the timber.

Between Bromham & Rowde Halt and Devizes the line crosses over two bridges. The first, Foxhanger Bridge across the Kennet and Avon Canal, was a girder bridge of three spans supported by cast iron columns filled with concrete. Over time the bridge showed signs of movement with the embankments giving cause for concern. Measures were taken to strengthen the bridge and its supports and by 1956 it could safely take locomotive-hauled trains. The second bridge crossed the A361 Bath Road diagonally and was called 'The Fish Bridge' as originally, from the side, the wrought-iron girders in its construction gave it the shape of a fish. In 1901 the bridge was replaced by a new lattice girder and steel brace structure.

The Stalking of Emily Lister

It was at the Fish Bridge in June 1889 that a tragedy occurred on the Devizes Line in a tale resembling an Agatha Christie novel.

Emily Lister had been close to eccentric schoolteacher Augustus Keeling, who had asked her to marry him. When she learned that he had spent time in an asylum she broke off the relationship and took up her new post as headmistress of a school in Devizes. Keeling followed her from Brighton and, in what might these days be termed a case of stalking, set about trying to win her back, including applying for a teaching post at her school!

Wanting to get away from him and Devizes for a little while, Miss Lister boarded a train for Bristol to see her parents in Birmingham. Keeling jumped on at the last moment and they were heard quarrelling in her compartment. Keeling asked her for money and when she refused he shot her twice in the head while the train was crossing the Fish Bridge. Miss Lister reached out of the carriage crying for help and as she did so, Keeling pushed her out, whereupon she fell down the embankment. An eyewitness on the train, Mr Brice, saw what was happening and with no communication cord to be pulled he opened the outside door of the carriage and tried to come to the aid of Emily by using the footboards to reach her compartment. The train's inspector, Mr Upchurch, saw Mr Brice and stopped the train.

Emily Lister was found, bloody but alive, on the lineside by a permanent way man who, with the aid of a plasterer working nearby, got her to hospital. In a sad twist of fate, though the two shots to the head were not critical, the fall from the train damaged one of her eyes so badly that it had to be removed. As for Keeling, his badly battered body was found further down the line, where he had jumped from the train. His body was buried in a pauper's grave after no relations came forward. Once recovered, Miss Lister went back to teaching.

Devizes to Patney and Chirton

Reaching Devizes station at 400 feet above sea level, two-thirds of the way down the line, you would see the Avon Vale to the north-west and the Vale of Pewsey to the south. The station was situated in a shallow cutting at the foot of Devizes Castle. Always large, over time it grew.

An early photo of Devizes station, circa early 1900, showing the overall roof. (Lens of Sutton)

The later, much changed, Devizes station, 1958. (Milepost 92½)

After Devizes became a through station it had twelve sidings serving a goods shed, an engine shed and various loading bays. One siding ended inside the tunnel under Devizes Castle, giving the impression that the tunnel was double-track. The station itself had two platforms covered by a roof and a lattice girder footbridge with a corrugated-iron roof spanned the two tracks. Two signal boxes sited at the end of the goods shed and at the tunnel mouth were later replaced by a single signal box next to the main platform building. Devizes had 1st and 2nd Class waiting rooms, a booking office, a parcels office, toilets and stores.

In 1874 the broad gauge track was converted to standard gauge and with the new-found space on the trackbed, the 'unofficial' platform on the down side was widened and brought into proper passenger use. It was also extended along with the original platform on the up side. By 1897 more sidings had been added in the goods yard and opposite the station on the up side. These new sidings were long enough to hold long rakes of up to 70 goods wagons.

In 1907 track was renewed and the up platform was curved and extended. Stables were built a year later for the GWR Horse Department and the cattle pens and coal pens were rail-served as well. 1909–10 saw platform canopies replace the roof and a new large footbridge was built, again, replacing the old one. Both flights of steps for the new footbridge were built facing in the down direction. A new platform was also brought into use on the outside of the down platform making this into an island. Around this time Devizes reached its peak. Traffic rose during the war years and by the Second World War GWR expresses hauled by *Castle Class* locomotives could be seen on the line.

Leaving Devizes on the stretch to Hungerford, the line travels under Devizes Castle through Devizes Tunnel. It was originally built for two tracks but except for the siding mentioned above it was always single-track. The tunnel was 570 feet long and 40 feet wide and was built on a 20° curve. The tunnel entrances either end were beautifully crenellated at the wish of the castle's owner.

Leaving the eastern end the line travelled under a footbridge after which in a little while it arrived at the delightfully named Pans Lane Halt. This was not unlike Semington Halt, and was built in part to serve the nearby Roundway Hospital. At 208 feet, long enough for a rail motor or an auto train, it had a small waiting hut. The Wiltshire United Dairy in Pans Lane sent its London output from Devizes, as Pans Lane was too small to cope with it.

The Devizes line then joined the GWR Reading–Westbury line at Patney & Chirton Junction near the village of Stert, continuing to run alongside the GWR line for about a mile through some passing loops and sidings before the station of Patney & Chirton was reached. Originally this was going to be called 'Patney Bridge' but before opening had its name changed to avoid any confusion with the London station of 'Putney Bridge'!

The station opened on 1st October 1900. A large island platform served the Devizes line on one side and the main line on the other. Moderately sized platform buildings with large canopies were built for passenger use and a long footbridge linked the main line platform, island platform and a public footpath on the far side of the Devizes line. In 1909 another platform was built opposite the Devizes line platform which was used for military traffic, serving the growing army presence on Salisbury Plain. If anything the station was too big since, apart from the military traffic, most people using it came from the local area.

The End of the Line

In August 1961 there was a major landslide on the GWR Reading–Westbury line between Patney & Chirton and Lavington. There had been trouble with this stretch of line because of movement and embankment subsidence for many years and work to strengthen it was ongoing. With all traffic from this main line being rerouted via Devizes, passenger and train levels more than doubled. During this diversion famous trains like the *Cornish Riviera Express*, *Torbay Express*, *Royal Duchy* and the *Mayflower* used the line. The pastime of train spotting enjoyed a surge of popularity amongst small boys. Unfortunately, so much traffic on the line caused nearby residents to complain about the noise! But the people on the Devizes line were to be cruelly let down. After the diversion was over and normal service was resumed, cuts on the line began.

A bridge carries the old track bed of the Devizes line over a farm road near Bromham & Rowde. (Author)

The Devizes line was due for closure in 1965, though many had seen this coming long before. Though the *Flying Scotsman* came through in October 1963 hauling a rake of Pullman Coaches on a rail tour, steam-hauled trains and freight ceased in 1964 to be replaced by two- and three-car DMUs for passenger use. The Devizes line was perhaps seen as a curiosity or a luxury: it linked two main lines but did not actually go anywhere. It had survived long enough to fall into the hands of British Rail and this is where the story ends.

Many saw British Rail as wanting to get rid of the line as quickly as possible. For if passenger numbers were the be-

The west portal of Devizes Tunnel now shows its new use as the entrance to a shooting range. (Author)

all and end-all then it seemed British Rail was going to make sure that those numbers fell. First the Sunday service was axed. Next, under the guise of a new timetable trains began arriving at the exchange stations after the connecting trains had already left and after having been held for almost half an hour at Devizes for no apparent reason! The halts were closed, track was lifted and Devizes station was left with a single line serving a single platform. Even before the line closed, scrap merchants and lifting gangs were already picking over the remains.

The people on the line lodged enough objections to its

closure that the line was to remain open until they had all been heard officially. But this was only a stay of execution and bought the line another year, which was perhaps just a slow death. The last public train ran on 16th April 1966.

There was a brief flurry of activity in June at the Holt end of the line on the thirteenth anniversary of the Coronation. The Royal Train arrived with the Queen and Prince Philip aboard on a tour of their Duchy Estate in Somerset. The train was hauled by a *Western* diesel hydraulic and was stabled on the branch overnight. A second *Western* arrived soon after to power the heating coach, at which point the lead engine was released to travel the Devizes line to Patney and from there to Westbury. This was perhaps the only time such a locomotive travelled over the line. The next day the Royal Train left for Castle Cary. Perhaps it was fitting that the Queen should be one of the last people on the line and afterwards a copy of the obituary of the line in *The Holt Magazine* was sent to her. This caused enough of a stir for the story to make at least one broadsheet newspaper.

The last trains over the line were of course the demolition trains that set about clearing the route during 1967. Not even the Fish Bridge survived, being dismantled to make way for a new dual carriageway. The approach embankments can still be seen, complete with the odd bridge over farmers' roads. The course of the old line is clearly marked on OS maps. Devizes station is now a large car park and can be reached via the telltale Station Road. The tunnel was sealed up long ago to make a local shooting range, the view of the castle above it now all but obscured by trees.

11
A Tale of Bacon and Two Halts

The Calne Branch

If you were looking at a map of the county of Wiltshire you would see that Calne is about the same distance from Devizes and Chippenham. The towns would make the points of a triangle located in the top left half of the county.

Though only six miles long, the line to Calne was in many ways the quintessential branch line. It served two stations or halts between Chippenham and Calne. The neat little GWR rail motors and auto trains became typical on the line. But its short length did not detract from the solid reputation it gained over time. In fact, such was its usage at its peak, especially for freight, that it often punched well above its weight.

Perhaps more than anything else, that weight could be measured in bacon! As well as the bacon factory at Chippenham, Calne had C. & T. Harris Ltd, one of the biggest bacon producers in the country. Such was the reputation of Harris's bacon that it was sent to Bristol, Leicester, Cardiff, London, Manchester, Newcastle, Southampton and York to name but some destinations. To keep the production line going vast supplies were brought in, of such essentials as salt and coal.

Passenger traffic was quite healthy as well. With RAF bases at Yatesbury, Compton Bassett and Lyneham, service personnel used the line and base stores were sent by rail to keep these establishments running. Just like the Devizes Branch in the previous chapter, the Calne Branch lasted long enough to be swallowed up by British Rail and see DMUs running over the line, before it fell victim to Dr Beeching.

In The Beginning

Like so many other towns and villages in Wiltshire, Calne was served by a canal, the Wiltshire and Berkshire Canal to be exact. But eventually the canal's speed of transportation appeared too slow to keep the bacon factory and other local concerns going. It seemed only natural to the people of Calne that the railway was the answer to their problem.

First off was an idea by the London, Bristol and South Wales Direct Railway in 1845 for a line from Maidenhead to Chippenham that would pass through the centre of Calne. This would have entailed the demolition of many buildings in the town and in the end this scheme came to nothing. But a special meeting presided over by the mayor resolved to attract a railway to Calne, to join the GWR at or near Chippenham station, the only dissenting voice coming from a man with a large stake in the canal, and so 'The Calne Railway Company' was born.

On a visit to the United States in 1847 to study techniques there, George Harris, owner of the bacon factory, had seen how ice could improve the manufacturing process. Returning home, his own business was beginning to boom, and he saw that the canal was not able to supply the quantities of ice, coal and salt to keep up with the demand. It should come as no surprise, then, to see that three members of the Harris family were on the board of the

Calne Railway Company, and that the Harris family subscribed more than half the money for it!

Parliamentary approval was given and the Act for the railway was passed on 15th May 1860 to raise £35,000 in capital and a further £11,600 in loans. James Baird Burke was hired as engineer for the project. Being such a short line there was not a great deal of construction work involved: the largest obstacle was the Avon, which was crossed by a heavily braced eight-span wooden bridge. A steel bridge of two spans on a brick pier would later replace this. Good quality stone for the roads, ballasting, track bed and other smaller bridges on the route came from the land of Mr Benjamin Bailey, a corn dealer and miller in Calne. The first train along the Branch ran on 29th October 1863, carrying what else but 100 pigs!

The line opened to passengers on 3rd November. For this event an unofficial holiday was held in Calne and the shops were closed as a military band played and paraded through the town in uniform. So many people turned up to ride the first train that many had to be left behind: in the end the train set off with close to a thousand people on board!

The Calne Railway Company never owned locomotives. Instead it had an agreement with the GWR that they run the line for just over half of the profits, and though the line was built as broad gauge, as was standard in the area at the time, by 1874 it had been converted to standard gauge. The work to achieve this seemingly began on a Friday evening and was completed by the following Monday! By 1892, the railway was dissolved into the GWR in its entirety.

In 1865 plans were drawn up for a north–south railway line through Wiltshire which would have run from Malmesbury, just passing Calne on its course, so it seemed obvious that the two railways should meet. Plans were drawn up for a quarter-mile extension from the end of the line at Calne to the Malmesbury route. Though an act was passed for this new Wiltshire railway, nothing came of it.

The Line in Detail

At Chippenham the GWR would have a sizeable base of operations and it played a big part in the history of the railways in the West Country. The Works included a small locomotive works that later became a bacon factory, and the main home for the famous Westinghouse Brake and Signal Company that by 1938 employed 2,700 people. Both plants had their own sidings. The station itself opened on 31st

The building that was Brunel's site office outside Chippenham station is now preserved. (Author)

*Very possibly a Calne train at Chippenham station, looking east, 1951.
(P J Garland Collection)*

May, 1841 and was designed, like so many other stations in
the area, by Brunel.

It had a single main line platform but, with the opening of
the extension lines to Weymouth and Salisbury between 1856
and 1857, the station was enlarged. This included a new
down bay platform for Weymouth trains and a vast roof.
Another bay platform for 'up' trains was then built for the
line to Calne. Perhaps bizarrely these 'bay platforms' were
not typical, but used opposite ends of the same island
platform and the same piece of track; the up main line ran on
the other side of the island. This was because each end of this
platform was controlled by its own signal box. So halfway
down an island platform serving two 'separate lines' sat
back-to-back buffers blocking the same track! By the
beginning of the 1900s the overall roof had been removed.

131

By the 1960s things had declined enough at Chippenham for rationalisation to take place. The 'up' bay line was lifted first, then the 'down' Weymouth bay line was next to go. The platform was then tidied up and the down main line was moved over to it in 1976. This gives us the Chippenham station we have today with one island platform. The buildings on the old down main line platform, though, are preserved and are listed.

Freight was major traffic at Chippenham and, aside from private sidings for the bacon factory and signal works, there were many more for storing wagons. Also present was a sizeable goods shed and engine shed. By 1981, however, goods traffic ceased from here and the last sidings were removed by 1984.

Leaving Chippenham travelling east, after the last goods sidings the line to Calne curves away to the south opposite the Chippenham Gas Works and another engine shed. Once past this curve it runs pretty much straight for two-thirds of the distance. Only in its last two miles did it begin to curve to follow the line of the Wiltshire and Berkshire Canal.

The first thing of note on the line was the Black Bridge across the Avon. It was originally, as noted above, a blackened wooden structure that went on to be replaced by a steel one in 1920. Shortly after this came the first halt on the line at Stanley Bridge. Interestingly, the GWR often spelt Halt the French way – *Halte* – at some of the smaller stops on its territory.

Located near Pound Farm, where the line began a series of curves, Stanley Bridge Halt was a very small stop built of timber and earth covered in gravel and had a small hut as a waiting room. Like Black Dog Halt, the other stop on the line, it was not built at the opening of the line but added later when the GWR began running rail motors on the line. It was opened in April 1905. Though passenger numbers from here were never very large, milk traffic was often such that, with the halt being unstaffed, a porter had to be sent from Chippenham to guard the churns in the evening, waiting for the next train.

The line then crossed over the Wiltshire and Berkshire Canal and a road bridge called Black Dog Bridge carried it over the Chippenham road, before arriving at Black Dog Halt. This station was built, not for the public but for the Marquess of Lansdowne who, seeing that the line passed along the edge of his Bowood estate, asked the Calne Railway Company to build him a siding from which he could supply his estate. The company agreed in 1870 and entered a financial agreement with him. A temporary platform had already been built here for passengers for the Bowood Fete on his land so this siding was seen as nothing out of the ordinary. However, Colonel Rich from the Board of Trade, when inspecting the halt before its opening, noted that a tree obscured the signal!

Once put right, parcels and goods were collected daily. The station was improved with the provision of a large waiting hut with a booking office and waiting room. A second siding was added at the end of the 19th century. Stables were provided for the transport of the Marquess's horses and a large loading dock was used for coal, grain, timber and even, later on, motor vehicles. To be the stationmaster at Black Dog Halt was probably a nice job as it came with many perks. The Marquess provided him with a large rent-free house in a low cutting surrounded by trees and shrubbery, free coal and the Marquess even helped pay his wages! To all intents and purposes the station remained a private one: while in GWR hands the Marquess banned a name board at the station until as late as 1951. Though until then he would let 'lesser' people use it, it was not listed in any timetable until 1952 and passengers wanting to alight

GWR auto train pulling into Black Dog Halt, 1955. (Millbrook House Ltd)

there could not buy a ticket for Black Dog Halt, but instead had to book to Calne.

When the then stationmaster retired in 1930 the GWR, not finding enough revenue to justify a replacement, terminated the agreement with the Marquess. Instead a lowly porter was employed and interestingly, one of the conditions of this new post was that the porter was not allowed to air any political views! 'Stationmasters' privileges' were withdrawn from the halt and the house rented out – only to be subsequently purchased by the same lowly porter. Along with the general run-down of the place the second siding was withdrawn and it became an unstaffed halt in 1960. Though the remaining siding was still used, all goods traffic ceased from here in 1963.

After Black Dog Halt the line ran via a couple more curves into Calne and a hive of freight activity. The town of Calne can trace its history as far back as the late 10th century while that of the meat business C. & T. Harris that saved the town and its economy can be traced back to 1770.

Emerging from a cutting into the station the line ran to one bay platform and in 1886 the station had four sidings serving a goods shed and a little engine shed. By 1923 the station began to expand to the south and had increased to eight sidings, many with concrete floors for washing out the wagons. Long bays and docks were built for loading and off-loading supplies and cattle. At its peak the goods yard could hold 174 full wagons. A sixteen-lever signal box was built to control all the movements in the yard.

By 1936 the layout had been extended by several hundred feet into more sidings to serve a factory built after the First World War. This took by-products from the main bacon factory to make products like fertiliser and chemicals for the soap and medical industries. Calne's population

Calne station in 1949, looking away from the end of the line. (Joe Moss Collection)

increased from 2,500 in 1861 to more than 6,500 in 1961.

By the 1920s more than 100,000 pigs were being slaughtered in Calne every year. The end product left the station in specially branded railway vans which were often coupled to the back of passenger trains.

The station itself expanded and was improved to handle the increasing passenger traffic, especially the RAF personnel using it, and in 1942 the platform was lengthened to handle eight-coach trains. During the Second World War the station's revenue reached its peak. The level of staff here topped around the 40 mark and it was not unknown for daily receipts to reach £1,000! The revenue from outward-going parcels was also impressive: in the Bristol Division, it was second only to Bristol Temple Meads! At its peak the total revenue from C. & T. Harris was £1,000 a month.

The nearby RAF bases also brought a lot of trade, especially RAF Lyneham which brought in and sent everything from men to engines to wrecked aircraft to motor vehicles through Calne. Milk was another commodity and a special service run by A.I. Hillier collected from the many farms in the area and delivered the milk to Calne.

The GWR also considered another railway link from Calne to Marlborough and, to see if such a scheme could be justified, it ran a motor coach service between the two towns from 1904 until 1932. No railway resulted from this, though.

The End of the Line

The end of the Calne Branch could be attributed to two things: motor transport and the rail strike of 1955 that forced a lot of rail traffic on to the roads. During the strike C. & T. Harris had to send most of its meat by road and it seems continued to do so. The strike also hit passenger numbers: in 1952 the branch carried 300,000 passengers; by 1959, this had fallen to 98,000. The parcel traffic fared even worse, falling from 500,000 to just 171,000 parcels. For a different reason, coach companies gained most of the passenger traffic from the RAF bases in the area. Weekend rail tickets, ideal for servicemen on leave, were not sold at Calne station. Such tickets were only issued by the time the management saw the writing on the wall but then it was too late.

A new swimming baths opened in Chippenham and this brought some traffic, but not enough. Conversion to diesel took place in 1959 and the Branch was operated by two- or three-coach DMUs, sometimes with a parcel van attached to the rear. By 1962 traffic had declined to the point that many services were cut including the Sunday service. By 1963 only one freight train ran each day and this stopped completely in November. Passenger traffic still ran, bucking the countrywide trend for freight to outlive it on other such lines.

British Rail and Branch staff argued bitterly about its future and disagreed on almost everything from passengers carried to its revenue. The latter became the most contested fact as BR's accountants claimed the revenue was only a third of what the staff claimed! But daily passenger numbers were now entering single digit territory. Calne was a shadow of its former self with one line and platform still in existence. The excuse for eventually closing the line was that the permanent way was worn out and to keep the line open would have required complete renewal. What they would have been loath to say was that they had allowed it to wear out in the first place!

East end of Chippenham station where the Calne line branched off right in the distance. (Author)

Tom Fraser, the Minister for Transport at the time, consented to the closing of the Calne Branch if adequate bus services existed. Shortly after, more bus services were added! The last day of passenger service was 18th September 1965. Hundreds of tickets had been sold for this last day of operation and the train was packed! As it ran between Calne and Black Dog Halt it exploded 102 detonators on the track, one for every year of the Branch's life.

The only remnants of the line are some earthworks and embankments. Entering Calne by the A3102 from Bromham and Rowde you come almost at once to Station Road, which leads to an industrial estate and another private road beside it. Continuing on this road leads to a low office building where the old station is now, yes, you've guessed it ... a car park!

The site of Calne station is now a car park. (Author)

12
In the Shadow of an Abbey

The Malmesbury Branch

'The Abbey on the Hill' at Malmesbury, dating back to a monastery from AD 640. The former station site lies in a little valley behind it. (Author)

'Malmesbury,' the poet John Betjeman said, 'was a city set on a hill that could not be hid.' Without doubt, it is one of the most picturesque towns in Wiltshire. Its abbey sitting high up on a hill overlooking the town dates as far back as

AD 640. It once boasted a spire taller than Salisbury Cathedral and had 16 chapels. Pilgrims came from all over the country to worship here and it is said that fragments of the Crown of Thorns were kept there. It was around this abbey that the early town became something of an island surrounded by the Avon and its lesser tributaries. Since then it has expanded down the hill but never outgrowing it. It was also at the abbey that a monk, brother Elmer, determined to fly, affixed wings to his arms and legs and leapt from one of its towers. It is recorded that he broke his legs but lived to see another mass!

Railway passengers arriving in Malmesbury, like the pilgrims and the monks of medieval times would have done so in the shadow of the abbey high on the hill. Like Devizes, Calne and other such market towns in Wiltshire, Malmesbury was a town filled with folk who wanted the railway to come to them.

The Malmesbury Railway

To begin with, it was the Midland Railway that was going to bring the railway to Malmesbury, or in fact through it. This was a marked departure for the Midland but, wanting a slice of the Wiltshire pie so to speak, they had a scheme to extend their 'Stonehouse and Nailsworth Railway' under the name of 'The Wiltshire and Gloucestershire Railway'. This line would run from Nailsworth through Tetbury and Malmesbury to Christian Malford on the GWR Main Line to Bristol, perhaps reasoning that if they got this far then they would be able to reach Salisbury and the South Coast.

This scheme was authorised through an Act of Parliament in 1864 but a year later another act granted the building of 'The North and South Wiltshire Railway'. This was to run from Malmesbury through Christian Malford, past Calne (as mentioned in the last chapter) and on to the Berkshire and Hampshire Extension Railway, which later became a GWR route. At it turned out, neither of these schemes came to fruition. The GWR and Midland Railway came to a negotiated peace and agreed not to 'invade each other's space'. Although work is said to have been started on the Wiltshire and Gloucestershire line it was soon abandoned.

So for the time being Malmesbury was left without a railway. But in July 1872 the local people got their way and an Act was passed that paved the way for the building of 'The Malmesbury Railway'. Though not able to raise all the funds themselves, they went into a partnership with the GWR who agreed to fund half the cost of £60,000 and to run the railway thereafter. Building began on 8th July 1874 and the line was completed on 17th December 1877. It was totally absorbed into the GWR on 1st July 1892.

The Line in Detail

Like the Calne Branch in the previous chapter, the Malmesbury Branch was only a short one of just over six miles. It originally began at Dauntsey on the GWR main line but after 1933 this all changed when the first half of the line was closed and the station of Little Somerford on the Bristol and South Wales Direct Railway not far away was used instead.

Dauntsey station was within a stone's throw of Dauntsey lock on the Wiltshire and Berkshire Canal. Here there was a creamery, brickworks and the Peterborough Arms public house but the village was only a very small one. The station itself was conventional enough with platforms either side of the main line and sidings either end serving as a goods yard. However, when the Malmesbury line was opened the end of the up platform was turned into a bay platform for the new line to run into behind it. Interestingly, at the point where the footbridge and road bridge crossed the main line, at the base of the support the platform slopes down and then back up to form a double ramp, as if to indicate where one platform ended and the other one began.

As the Malmesbury line leaves Dauntsey it curves away sharply to the right through a junction and while this curve is double-track, it quickly narrows into a single line. The junction from the bay platform served both tracks, one into the bay and one onto the up main line as well as going straight on to serve a long siding into the up end goods yard. Passing over Swallet Gate Bridge, Poole's Bridge and Dauntsey Road Crossing, the first station on the single line to Malmesbury was Great Somerford Halt.

This halt was built near St Peter & St Paul's church and Brook Farm and though classed as a halt it was actually nearer to being a station. It was made of wood and timber and had a large timber booking office and waiting room. At the turn of the century it had a staff of five and handled almost 3,000 tons of goods a year for which a short reversible siding was laid. Milk traffic here alone accounted for up to 100 cartloads of churns a day. It was named simply Somerford until January 1903 when Little Somerford on the Bristol and South Wales Direct Railway opened. By May 1922 staffing at this station ended and the siding was taken out of use.

Continuing onwards, the Malmesbury Branch travelled under the Bristol and South Wales Direct Railway, near to Little Somerford station. After this, Malmesbury would have been the next and last stop on the line. However, in July 1933, Little Somerford became the new starting point of the Malmesbury Branch and the stretch between Dauntsey and the Bristol and South Wales Direct Railway was taken out of service, which cut the length of the line from six miles to just under four miles.

The journey to this point began when the Bristol and South Wales Direct Railway was opened in 1903 as a shorter route to the Severn Tunnel from Swindon on the GWR main line. To carry material for the new line it was decided to lay a connection from it to the Malmesbury Branch. In 1933, to save money it was decided to make this spur a permanent fixture and Little Somerford was altered to make it the new beginning of the journey to Malmesbury. Though the necessary work to do this was completed by February 1933, legal technicalities prevented the authorities from closing the original Dauntsey section until July.

Rather oddly, when the curves at Dauntsey were lifted after 1933, the bay platform retained its track until 1956! And the timber that made the station of Great Somerford was sold for a mere £10! A short stretch of the Dauntsey section's track on the other side of the Bristol and South Wales Direct Railway Bridge, before it met the new spur, was kept to store wagons until this too was lifted in 1959.

So now, beginning at Little Somerford the Malmesbury Branch would run west out of the station for a little way. There was nothing 'little' about this station, having up and down platforms that were served by two long passing loops leaving the two main lines free for through running. The western end of the up loop, where a little siding or 'neck' was located, was converted into the curve to Malmesbury simply by carrying the siding on parallel to the up track until it curved round to join the 'old' Malmesbury line. There were at least four other sidings here, including a goods yard with a shed and cattle pens. A long footbridge was built to stretch over all four tracks between the platforms.

Further along the branch we come to Malmesbury Tunnel, which was 105 yards long. It was a very basic tunnel and had straight sheer sides with a curved ceiling. Leaving this tunnel into Malmesbury station the abbey would be behind, high up on the hill. The station was built just north of the town and parallel to the Avon. However, photographs taken of the station from the end of the line often make it look as if the abbey overlooked the station from the opposite end.

The station was quite a large one, with a long parallel siding on the right serving a goods shed and a long parallel siding further along on the left serving an engine shed. A second running line passed through the station and was used for stabling and shunting. The single platform and

Malmesbury station, 1949, with the engine shed on the right. (Joe Moss Collection)

Malmesbury station, 1948, with the Abbey up on the hill in the background. (P J Garland Collection)

station itself were on the left with the platform building being constructed of stone and made to look medieval with tall chimneys and bay windows to blend with its surroundings. Both tracks through the station merged into one that ended at buffers a few metres further.

Goods traffic here was similar to that from other small Wiltshire towns: mainly cattle, milk and coal left Malmesbury. To begin with, passenger traffic saw six trains each way on weekdays with more services on market days. The early 1900s brought the high point for passenger traffic on the line with more than 20,500 tickets sold. By 1933 this had fallen to 6,000. Freight likewise declined to about half what it had been in the same time span.

147

The End of the Line

Traffic was never huge over the Malmesbury Branch. Even halving its length after 1933 could not save it. Increasing road traffic after the Second World War saw the train services cut back until 1951 when on 19th September all passenger traffic ended. A fall in Malmesbury's population (by over 200 in 60 years) did not help either. Freight continued to run until October 1962. By this time steam had ended on the line and instead all freight traffic was hauled by a slow-moving 0-6-0 diesel shunter. However, the line was sometimes used to test DMUs and with much of the line and its infrastructure hanging on, though overgrown and dilapidated, DMUs packed with railway enthusiasts sometimes visited on railway tours.

Still standing after all these years, the former GWR Malmesbury engine shed is now a tyre and exhaust centre. (Author)

Dauntsey station still remains, though the track layout has been changed to reflect modern times with the single line now moved over to the island platform. Little Somerford, despite its size, is now just a memory and passengers passing through on a fast High Speed Train would not even guess that a station had existed there. Great Somerford has disappeared completely though the track bed still remains.

At Malmesbury it is a little different and a gem for railway archaeologists can still be found. Making one's way behind the magnificent abbey, then descending some steps to cross the Avon and a lovely little weir on a footbridge, you come to a small picnic area. On the right is a public footpath that was once the old track bed, now a nature reserve. On the left and next to the picnic area is a rather incongruous trading estate with some small factory outlets, business offices and workshops. This is the site of the old station area. If you walk away from the abbey to the end of this industrial estate you would find, standing in remarkable condition with its original doors, the old engine shed still being used for mechanical purposes: it's now a tyre fitters and garage!

Opening and Closing Dates of Lines/Stations in this book

(The Opening Date and the Final Closing Date for all kinds of Service)

Line	Opened	Final Closure
Midland & South Western Junction Railway		
Swindon, Marlborough & Andover Railway	1881	
Swindon & Cheltenham Extension Railway	1883	1961
Marlborough and Grafton Railway	1898	
Swindon & Highworth Railway	1883	1962
London & South Western Railway		
Grateley to Bulford Camp	1901	1963
Salisbury (Milford Goods)	1847	1967
Salisbury (Fisherton Street)	1859	
Great Western Railway		
Salisbury	1856	1991
Devizes	1857	
(through line)	1862	1966
Calne	1863	1965
Malmesbury	1877	1962

150

Line	Opened	Final Closure
Salisbury Market House Branch	1859	1964
Military Camp Railways around Salisbury		
Fovant Camp	1915	
Codford Camp	1914	1922–4
Heytesbury Branch	1916	1923–6

Heritage Railway Line and Museum in Wiltshire

Swindon & Cricklade Railway
Blunsdon Station, Tadpole Lane, Blunsdon, Swindon SN25 2DA
Tel (weekends only): 01793 771615; Website: http://www.swindon-cricklade-railway.org/
Swindon & Cricklade Railway is a standard gauge heritage railway providing a round trip of four miles with vintage steam, diesel-hauled trains and DMUs.

STEAM – Museum of the Great Western Railway
Fire Fly Avenue, Swindon SN2 2EY
Tel: 01793 466646; Website: http://www.steam-museum.org.uk/Pages/Home.aspx
email: steammuseum@swindon.gov.uk
This museum is in a restored Grade II listed railway building, at the old Swindon railway works in Swindon. Inside, you can discover the story of the Great Western Railway, the people who built and worked for it, and see some famous locomotives.

151

Bibliography

Books

Along Country Lines, P. Atterbury (David & Charles, 2005)

Basingstoke to Salisbury, V. Mitchell & K. Smith (Middleton Press, 1991, 1999)

Branch Lines of West Wiltshire, V. Mitchell & K. Smith (Middleton Press, 1993)

Branch Lines of Wiltshire, C. Maggs (Sutton, 1992)

British Railways Past & Present No.22: Wiltshire, Roose & Ballantyne (Past & Present Publications, 1994, 2002)

Brunel, J. Falconer (Ian Allan, 1995, 2005)

Brunel, The Man Who Built the World, S. Brindle (W&N, 2005)

Brunel's Britain, D. Beckett (David & Charles, 1980–2006)

Cheltenham to Andover, V. Mitchell & K. Smith (Middleton Press, 2000, 2002)

Complete British Railways Maps and Gazetteer from 1830–1981, C.J. Wignall (OPC, 1983)

Didcot to Swindon, V. Mitchell & K. Smith (Middleton Press, 2002)

Encyclopaedia of British Railway Companies, C. Awdry (PSL, 1990)

Fareham to Salisbury, V. Mitchell & K. Smith (Middleton Press, 1989, 2004)

Great Western Branch Lines: 1 – The South-West, M.S. Welch (Runpast Publishing, 2002)

GWR Country Stations, C. Leigh (Ian Allan, 1981, 1985, 2001)

GWR Then & Now, L. Waters (Ian Allan, 1994)

GWR to Devizes, R. Priddle & D. Hyde (Millstream Books, 1996)

LSWR West Country Lines Then and Now, M. Hawkins (D&C, 1993)

Main Line to the West Part One, J. Nicholas & G. Reeve (Irwell Press, 2004)

Midland and South Western Junction Railway, G. Maggs (David & Charles, 1967, 1980)

Midland and South Western Junction Railway, T.B. Sands (Oakwood Press, 1959, 1975, 1979, 1990)

Midland and South Western Junction Railway, Bridgeman & Barnsley (Tempus Publishing, 1994)

Midland and South Western Junction Railway Vol. One, D. Bartholomew (Wild Swan, 1982)

Newbury to Westbury, Mitchell, Smith & Robertson (Middleton Press, 2001)

Rail Atlas Great Britain & Ireland, S. K. Baker (OPC, 1977–2001)

Rail Centres: Swindon, C. Maggs (Ian Allan, 1983)

Railway Track Diagrams 3: Western, Jacobs & Yonge (Quail Map Co, 1989,1992, 2002, 2005)

Railway Track Diagrams 5: England South & London Underground, Jacobs & Yonge (Quail Map Co, 2002)

Salisbury to Westbury, V. Mitchell & K. Smith (Middleton Press, 1994)

Salisbury to Yeovil, V. Mitchell & K. Smith (Middleton Press, 1992)

Stonehenge Complete, C. Chippindale (Thames & Hudson, 1983,1994, 2004)

Swindon to Bristol, V. Mitchell & K. Smith (Middleton Press, 2002)

The Bulford Branch Line (P. A. Harding, 1991)

The Calne Branch, G. Tanner (OPC, 1972)

The Calne Branch, C. Maggs (Wild Swan, 1990)

The GWR Swindon to Bath Line, C. Maggs (Sutton, 2003)

The Great Western Railway, 150 Glorious Years, Whitehouse & St John Thomas (David & Charles, 1984)

Wiltshire, M. Child (Shire Publications, 1995)

Wiltshire Railways in Old Photographs, K. Robertson (Sutton, 1988, 1997)

Wiltshire Railway Stations, M. Oakley (Dovecote Press, 2004)

Magazines

Back Track Vol.3/No.3 (July–August 1989)

Railway Magazine (December 2002)

Maps

Bartholomew's Revised 'Half Inch' Map No.29: Salisbury Plain (1937)

OS Explorer 118: Shaftesbury (OS Maps, 1997)

OS Explorer 130: Salisbury & Stonehenge (OS Maps, 1997)

OS Explorer 156: Chippenham & Bradford-on-Avon (OS Maps, 2004)

OS Explorer 157: Marlborough & Savernake Forest (OS Maps, 2004)

OS Explorer 168: Stroud, Tetbury & Malmesbury (OS Maps, 1998, 2001)

OS Explorer 169: Cirencester & Swindon (OS Maps, 1998, 2005)

OS of England & Wales, No. 69: Cirencester & Swindon (D&C Reprint of First Edition from 1828)

OS of England & Wales, No. 77: Devizes (D&C Reprint of First Edition from 1817)

OS of England & Wales, No. 85: Salisbury & New Forest (D&C Reprint of First Edition from 1811)

Videos and DVDs

Great Western Branches and By-Ways (TVP)

The Lost Betjemans (Green Umbrella)

INDEX